RESOURCE-FUL CONSULTING

RESOURCE-FUL CONSULTING
Working with your Presence and Identity
in Consulting to Change

*Karen Izod and
Susan Rosina Whittle*

KARNAC

First published in 2014 by
Karnac Books Ltd
118 Finchley Road
London NW3 5HT

Copyright © 2014 by Karen Izod and Susan Rosina Whittle

The rights of Karen Izod and Susan Rosina Whittle to be identified as the authors of this work have been asserted in accordance with §§ 77 and 78 of the Copyright Design and Patents Act 1988.

All rights reserved. No part of this publication may be reproduced, stored in a retrieval system, or transmitted, in any form or by any means, electronic, mechanical, photocopying, recording, or otherwise, without the prior written permission of the publisher.

Illustrations © Isabel Milford, www.izzymilford.com

British Library Cataloguing in Publication Data

A C.I.P. for this book is available from the British Library

ISBN-13: 978-1-78220-041-3

Typeset by V Publishing Solutions Pvt Ltd., Chennai, India

Printed in Great Britain

www.karnacbooks.com

CONTENTS

LIST OF FIGURES — vii

LIST OF TABLES — ix

ACKNOWLEDGEMENTS — xiii

ABOUT THE AUTHORS — xv

INTRODUCTION — xvii
Karen Izod

CHAPTER ONE
Potential space — 1
Susan Rosina Whittle

CHAPTER TWO
Identity — 11
Karen Izod

CHAPTER THREE
Presence — 25
Susan Rosina Whittle

CHAPTER FOUR
Role space — 53
Karen Izod

CHAPTER FIVE
Practice — 63
Susan Rosina Whittle and Karen Izod

CHAPTER SIX
Change: developing resource-ful practice — 89
Karen Izod and Susan Rosina Whittle

CHAPTER SEVEN
Future developments — 119
Susan Rosina Whittle

APPENDIX — 129

WEB RESOURCES — 135

REFERENCES — 137

INDEX — 143

LIST OF FIGURES

FIGURE 1
Book structure — xxi

FIGURE 1.1
The Johari window — 3

FIGURE 1.2
P3C a potential space to … — 10

FIGURE 2.1
Mirroring — 18

FIGURE 2.2
Projection — 22

FIGURE 3.1
Presence intended and unintended — 42

FIGURE 3.2
Encounters and entanglements — 44

FIGURE 3.3
Presence and transference — 45

FIGURE 3.4
Presence as intervention — 50

FIGURE 4.1
Role configuration — 54

FIGURE 4.2 Realities of role configuration	55
FIGURE 4.3 Applying for role	60
FIGURE 5.1 Consulting cycle, a linear sequence of stages	65
FIGURE 5.2 Stages of the consulting cycle—the reality	65
FIGURE 5.3 Stages of the consulting cycle: preoccupations and neglect	66
FIGURE 5.4 P3C module themes and practice dynamics as stages of the consulting cycle	67
FIGURE 5.5 Dynamics of expertise and containment in the process of hiring and being hired	70
FIGURE 5.6 What do I see?	72
FIGURE 5.7 Taking risks with interventions	76
FIGURE 5.8 Attachment patterns	86
FIGURE 6.1 Ladder of inference	95
FIGURE 6.2 Drawing inferences	96
FIGURE 6.3 Inquiry and advocacy modes	101
FIGURE 6.4 Reputational risk	110
FIGURE 6.5 Angels and devils	116
FIGURE 7.1 Presence as intervention	121
FIGURE 7.2 What's on my radar?	124
FIGURE 7.3 Three narrative forms	127

LIST OF TABLES

ANALYTIC
Johari window analysis   4

BOX 1.1
Acting out   6

BOX 2.1
Introducing ourselves   14

BOX 2.2
Identities and meaning-making   16

ANALYTIC
What examples do you encounter?   16

ANALYTIC
Being recognised and helping myself be recognisable   19

BOX 2.3
Emotions generated/regulated in contracting   20

ANALYTIC
Emotions generated/regulated in contracting   21

ANALYTIC
Noticing emotional tendencies   23

ANALYTIC
Transferred emotion and role   24

BOX 3.1
Encountering colleagues   26

BOX 3.2
My presence   29

ANALYTIC
Presence traps   31

ANALYTIC
Confidence dynamics   35

ANALYTIC
Competition dynamics   37

ANALYTIC
Control dynamics   39

ANALYTIC
Presence index   40

ANALYTIC
Streams of presence   43

ANALYTIC
What I know about my presence   48

ANALYTIC
Expectations between task and role   57

ANALYTIC
Time lines (time to play)   59

ANALYTIC
Working out the me/not me   61

ANALYTIC
Consulting cycle preoccupations   66

TABLE 5.1
Mixed emotions at entry and contracting   69

ANALYTIC
Working with your competence and containment   70

BOX 5.1
Models of organisation and where attention is directed   71

ANALYTIC
Data preoccupations   73

BOX 5.2
What a change strategy should include   75

BOX 5.3
Strategies for working on inclusion and exclusion 78

BOX 5.4
Six maladaptive strategies for coping with uncertainty 79

ANALYTIC
Past the sell-by date 81

BOX 5.5
Evaluating consulting work 82

ANALYTIC
Evaluating your work 82

BOX 5.6
Assessing levels of change: perspectives from a resource-ful approach 84

ANALYTIC
Assessing levels of change 85

ANALYTIC
Assessing attachment patterns when working with evaluations and endings 87

ANALYTIC
The bystander 92

ANALYTIC
Star-trekking 93

ANALYTIC
Inferences 94

BOX 6.1
Two types of fallacy when drawing inferences 95

ANALYTIC
Drawing inferences 97

ANALYTIC
Data selection and interpretation 100

BOX 6.2
Advocacy > Inquiry 101

BOX 6.3
Control mechanisms 103

ANALYTIC
Working on control mechanisms 103

ANALYTIC
Which detective? 105

ANALYTIC
Crafting a professional narrative — 106

BOX 6.4
Working with narrative structures — 107

BOX 6.5
Kim's story — 108

ANALYTIC
Creating your own narrative — 109

ANALYTIC
Credibility and authority to work — 111

ANALYTIC
Analysing your reputational risk — 114

ANALYTIC
Working with your angels and devils — 116

BOX 7.1
The fashion for resilience — 120

TABLE 7.1
Nine categories to demonstrate use of "self-as-instrument" in practice — 122

ANALYTIC
Development analysis — 123

ANALYTIC
Plotting development needs — 124

BOX 7.2
Development in context — 124

ANALYTIC
My development in context — 125

BOX 7.3
Narrative plots — 126

ANALYTIC
Which narrative? — 128

BOX APP 1
P3C module themes — 129

BOX APP 2
P3C participant characteristics — 132

BOX APP 3
Layers of experience — 133

ACKNOWLEDGEMENTS

We would like to thank the many participants on our professional development programmes and workshops, and our clients with whom we work in consulting and coaching relationships. We think and learn in active engagement with others, and our approach to professional development emerges from the lived experiences, ups and downs, that we have encountered alongside our clients over twenty-five years of working in this field.

The Tavistock Institute of Human Relations has provided us with an institutional base from which to direct the Practitioner Certificate in Consulting and Change between 2009 and 2013. We appreciate and acknowledge the work and contribution of our professional partners at the Tavistock Institute, alongside its intellectual heritage and contemporary work which continues to influence us.

Karen Izod and
Susan Rosina Whittle

ABOUT THE AUTHORS

Karen Izod, MA, CQSW

KIzod Consulting, established in 1996 provides a platform for my work in collaborative enterprises with clients and fellow change consultants, academics, and researchers at local, national, and international level. I work with issues of risk and accountability, where clarity and direction are elusive and in situations which are often unpredictable. I am concerned with how relationships play out in organisations, between individuals, teams, and organisations, particularly across diverse political and stakeholder interests, and work to establish positive working relationships at times of conflict. My consulting and coaching bring me into developmental agendas in government and politics, financial services, higher education, industry and third sector organisations. I integrate creative media and experiential learning into my work particularly as a means of researching the dynamics of organisational dilemmas.

My educational work has involved me in designing programmes with and for The Tavistock Institute, Tavistock and Portman NHS Foundation Trust, and as bespoke courses for specific organisations. I am a Professional Partner at The Tavistock Institute, visiting lecturer/tutor on a number of Doctoral and Master's Degree programmes including the MSc in Coaching and Behavioural Change, Henley Business School, and MSc in Inter-professional Health and Social Care at Canterbury Christ Church University, and I lecture and run workshops widely. I have published on group and organisational dynamics, inter-professional relations, coaching and consulting practice, attachment and belonging, and am joint editor of *Mind-ful Consulting* (Karnac, 2009). I also write creatively and am a fledgling poet.

Dr Susan Rosina Whittle BA, MSc, PhD, MIC

For many years, I have combined my work as an independent consultant with professional development and educational roles for The Tavistock Institute, National School of Government, and UK universities. In my consultancy work, I specialise in helping clients to introduce new ways of thinking and working to address organisational needs and problems. I have consulted for directors, managers, change agents, consultants, teams, and groups in many sectors, including manufacturing, government, health, construction, philanthropy, and the prison service. Typical assignments include: consortium building in contexts of resource scarcity; loss of trust in multi-organisational initiatives; responding to externally driven culture change; and consulting to strategy options in contested contexts. Much of my work now is with internal and external organisation development and change consultants, helping them to craft an authoritative presence by enhancing their repertoires and sustaining their identities in tough working environments.

I have published in academic and practitioner journals, *Mind-ful Consulting* (Karnac, 2009) and *Changing Organizations from Within* (Gower, 2013). I have taught programs in organisation development, quality management, and research methods at Masters level in a number of universities and served as external examiner at Manchester and Brighton Business Schools. I am a Professional Partner at The Tavistock Institute. From 2001 to 2009 I held a core faculty role on The Tavistock Institute's Advanced Organisational Consultation Masters programme and until 2011 held a core faculty role on Birmingham University's MA in Leading Public Service Change and Organisational Development.

INTRODUCTION

Karen Izod

This is a book about consulting to organisations—consulting to the tasks and processes of change, where the self is an essential tool of consulting practice. Like any tool, bad practice can damage this instrument, the self, and like change, our language is in the present, it is continuous—doing, organising, changing, knowing, evaluating.

We are talking with, listening to, and working with consultants and change agents in our professional development programmes, in shadow-consultancy relationships, and in our own consulting engagements. Practitioners looking to re-vitalise their work through the Tavistock Institute Practitioner Certificate in Consulting and Change (P3C)[1] are beset with questions which generally place the "me" or the "I" at their core.

> "My beliefs about change are being challenged, I want to understand more about the different influences that shape my actions and re-actions".

> "I'm in a change process where I continually lose myself, I struggle to keep my own views and position in sight".

> "How can I know what works? I need to know more about how I do the work that I do".

> "What I don't understand is how change doesn't happen, even when it's clearly for the common good? I feel that I need to do something differently".

These questions, with their stated intentions to understand more, to know how to intervene, and account for what we do, illustrate how we as consultants get stuck in the ways that we think, and the things that we do. Stuckness and the need for change belong as much in the world of the consultant as the client, as we each bring influence to bear upon the other. We can be surprised when we discover that our behaviours are being shaped by the very dynamics we are in touch with in our clients, and when we lose sight of our own roles and identities. We can be thrown when what we know and rely upon in the face of change proves inappropriate or inadequate in the moment.

Experiences of surprise, of being thrown by situations, of things not being what we anticipate, are features of everyday organisational life, and a meeting point between what we might expect to happen and what actually takes place. So the platform from which we might be attempting to effect change in itself can be thought of as endlessly shifting, driven by instability (Weick & Quinn, 1999) and environmental turbulence (Emery & Trist, 1965, Owers, 2009).

These are situations when a firmer or more "secure base" (Bowlby, 1988) for practice becomes appealing, and when the resources at our disposal, the theories that we have in use (Argyris & Schon, 1974) and the experiences we have laid down, can feel inadequate to meet the challenges of consulting practice. Our concern, as consultants looking to develop reliable skills and practices, relates to the conditions that support an operational landscape firm enough to offer credibility and accountability for what we know and what we do, yet supple enough to move around the unpredictability, emergence and unfolding of change with an agility of lively ideas and repertoires. In our view, this has to encompass the taking of risks, and inevitably then, this means coping with anxiety, in ourselves and in our clients.

Why we are writing Resource-ful Consulting

These practice challenges were present in our minds as we designed the P3C programme (see Appendix). We offered a potential space (Winnicott, 1953) to explore and experiment with the conditions for consulting and change practice through the ideas of "front-stage/back-stage" (Goffman, 1959): front-stage, the experience of being mind-fully present with the client, in a visible consulting and change relationship; back-stage, the work that we do away from the client, through our own inner dialogues, our conversations and activities with colleagues.

We began considering these aspects of practice in *Mind-ful Consulting* (Whittle & Izod, 2009), a collection of edited stories from practitioners working within the Tavistock tradition. We emphasised the features of mindfulness as practice challenges:

- to be present in the moment, disentangling our attention from the past and the future
- to be alert to the complacency of routine and undermining of complexity
- to be aware of the limitations of restrictive mind-sets and the constraints for creativity they pose.

Our intention in writing this book is to create a similar potential space for exploration: stimulating questions about practice, and offering means to work through consulting dilemmas so as to continually shape the kind of resource that we can be, and can make available to our clients. Our attention is focussed on the practical and the vital. What keeps us and our clients stuck in unhelpful positions? How can we move on to embody the potential for, and promote the conditions for change? As we experiment with ways in which we as organisational change practitioners can develop our craft, we find an asset-based approach to consulting helps us to question, reveal and challenge the nature of "stuckness" in our own consulting practice, in our clients, and in organisational systems. Such an approach relies on our own capacities to be resource-ful:

to have the means to build, relate to, and play with the way we do things "lightly"—when the dynamics of change often involve loss and depletion (Marris, 1982), and contested power and responsibility (Hoggett, 2006).

Our premise for the book

Resource-ful Consulting places me—the consultant, my identities, and my capacity to be present—at the centre of change processes, through offering routes to develop practical skills, theoretical confidence and authoritative presence. This is far from a change formula. Instead we propose that all consulting work is mediated through my sense of self, and how I manage exchanges between my inner worlds of thoughts and feelings, and my outer world of roles and tasks. Specifically these include paying attention to—

- My identities—who am I, and who am I not at any one time?
- My presence—how much can I regulate my behaviour in the face of anxiety and complacency?
- My preoccupations—what am I usually in touch with, through my thoughts and feelings, and what do I habitually ignore or avoid?

We identified how these aspects of the professional self shape practice by analysing our experiences of directing the TIHR P3C Programme alongside the professional development programmes we design for our clients, and our consulting and shadow consulting activities.

Offering opportunities for experimentation and collaborative learning in Experiential Learning Labs, and in analytic and creative activities, the P3C programme revealed, in experienced and accomplished consultants: temptations to hide behind role, rather than explore different identities; wishes to disappear in anxiety provoking moments, rather than attend to them; tendencies to fall back on favourite solutions as a means of knowing, rather than face the emergent; and reluctance to notice how these shrink capacity for a functional and emotionally authentic engagement between consultant and client. The result is a diminished capacity for development and change.

In this book, we present narratives of how consultants are tripped up by, and feel trapped in these kinds of habitual and perpetual preoccupations. These "trip-trap" narratives derive from the ways that we (as directors) attempt to make sense of experiences that participants encounter in our programmes, including our constructed understanding in the moment, their own reported analyses of their experiences, and the issues that confront them in their practice.

We see these preoccupations surface in the Experiential Learning Labs, as in this example:

> I felt like an evacuee being sent off to the unknown to negotiate with the other group, I needed someone to come with me (no-one is paying much attention as he retells his story)

We hear them told as consulting stories, about being stuck in the history of an organisation or relationship with a colleague or client and unable to see things with fresh eyes, or always having to be the resilient, infallible, finder of solutions, struggling to work with an unknown future.

> It's a complex set of relationships: my consulting partner used to work for this client when she was at another consulting company. The client, and my partner, behave as if we are all part of her team, but this doesn't acknowledge my role as partner now. I don't see how I can step outside this web to take up a different kind of consulting role.

These narratives offer insights into how to identify and work with preoccupations to access and sustain the creative space that is needed for consulting practice. All too easily, this space can be eroded and with it the loss of potential for generating and regenerating change in ourselves, our clients and their organisations.

The model for Resource-ful Consulting that we offer, has at its origins, principles of learning from action and experience (Kolb, 1984) and the language that we use and the concepts that we draw on in our sense-making chime with a number of recognised approaches. Our approach and methodology are rooted in classic and contemporary Tavistock expertise in individual learning, group development, and organisational change.

In *Mind-ful Consulting* (Whittle & Izod, 2009) outlined earlier, we advocate an approach based upon mind-ful presence and attentiveness, and the challenge to routine. We draw upon inter-subjective developmental stances (Fonagy, Gergely, Jurist & Target, 2004; Bowlby, 1988; Bartholomew & Horowitz, 1991); and a relational understanding of individuals and groups in organisations and society, (Clarke, Hahn & Hoggett, 2009; Izod, 2009). We relate to a wide stream of thinking on contemporary consulting dilemmas (Whittle, 2013; CFAR).

Who is it for?

This book is for professionals working in consulting and developmental relationships with individual and organisational clients seeking to effect change. We expect that you have your own stories to tell and will be aware of some of the "trips and traps" that are part of your practice already.

If now is the time to take a step-back from your existing practice, to question and renew how you work, this book will invite you into a "playful" space to help you notice situations where you get stuck and have difficulty making sense of what might be going on. It will help you to check out your reliance on familiar routines and your favourite ways of thinking and doing and risk changing them.

Designed in a handbook format, our book provides theories and resources to guide the way you use yourself as an instrument (Cheung-Judge, 2001) for change, and help you reorganise yourself for the challenges of your consulting practice. Drawing upon our experiences of working with the professional development of consultants and change professionals over many years, *Resource-ful Consulting* aims to provide insights for learning and development professionals working at the edge of practice in their organisations.

What does the book cover?

The book is structured into seven chapters. Each chapter offers ways of thinking about, exploring, and practicing resource-ful consulting as outlined in Figure 1. We locate four core chapters, identity, presence, practice and change in between our inner worlds of thoughts, fantasies, feelings, and our outer words of tasks, behaviours and responsibilities. They are sequential: how we bring ourselves to our work through our identities and presence, influences our consulting practice. Preoccupations in our consulting practice indicate where and how we need to consider change. Interspersed between these four chapters we locate chapters on potential space and role space: spaces between the imagination and reality, where experimentation as a basis for resource-ful practice can reside.

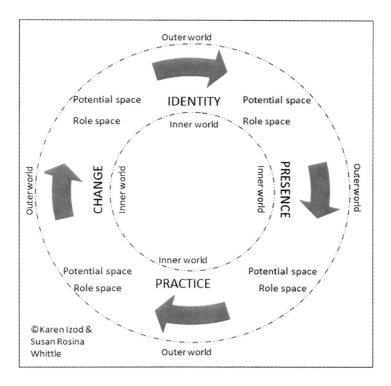

Figure 1. Book structure.

Chapter One: Potential space—is our invitation to you as readers, to take up the possibilities of exploring and experimenting. It takes us into a place of transition where we can catch unexpected glimpses of ourselves thinking and behaving differently. In such a space, we have the capacity to create new meanings for our experiences, and to reshape our habitual responses.

Chapter Two: Identity—how can I manage and experiment with aspects of my identity? This chapter addresses the question of "who I am" and "who I am not" at any one time so as to bring an awareness of how our identities can support or constrain our work as consultants and change practitioners. Paying active attention to the way we access our identities enables us to bring a more authentic, less cluttered self to the client, providing space for a broader repertoire of interventions. Describing three dynamic aspects of identity (recognition, regulation, and revelation) which can preoccupy consultants in their interactions with colleagues and clients alike, we illustrate how our identities act as filters through which we access resources: stories, places, cultures that help bring meaning to our experiences.

Chapter Three: Presence—how can I manage and experiment with aspects of my presence? In this chapter we turn to presence and why it matters, addressing the need to own our presence, to influence and maybe change how others encounter us. Describing three powerful authority dynamics that shape presence (confidence, competition, and control), we consider intended and unintended presence, and explain how presence is impacted by thoughts and feelings that transfer across time and place. Throughout this section, we invite you to explore what you know about your own presence, and how to think about presence as an intervention that can help or hinder work with your clients and colleagues.

Chapter Four: Role space—concerns itself with professional and organisational role, both as a resource and a mediator between individual, group, and organisation in consulting practice. Roles can act as the movers of our identities, and the shapers of our presence, and at the same time can impose expectations—the shoulds and oughts of what we do and how to do it. We work with the idea of roles "in the wings" of our practice, there to be taken up and crafted in such a way to bring ourselves to work with the resources afforded by identity and presence.

Chapter Five: Practice—explores the preoccupations we encounter that shape our practice in our engagements with clients. Using the consulting cycle as a means of locating practice preoccupations, we offer theories and models to help make sense of the dynamics associated with: entry and contracting, gathering data, designing interventions, learning and regression, and evaluation and endings. Working from practitioners' narratives of consulting in each of these stages, we make links with the dynamics of identity and presence encountered.

Chapter Six: Change—is about doing things differently, acting upon ideas and insights, facing preoccupations with intent to work on them. In this section we revisit those preoccupations with authority that shape presence, (confidence, competition, and control) and those preoccupations which relate to our identities (recognition, regulations, and revelation) and offer ways to start changing preoccupations into assets to craft a more resourceful presence. Much of our work involves experiential learning, that is, learning from your experience rather than from mine. We cannot replicate that here, in this format, but give a taste of some of the activities that you might want to try with others.

Chapter Seven: Future development—is an opportunity to bring together your insights and evaluations in a development agenda for your own professional practice. We outline a set of capabilities we use to help practitioners hone their use of "self-as-instrument" (Cheung-Judge, 2001) together with ways of identifying continuing professional needs.

Settling down to work of this kind requires space—and curiosity.

Chapter One is the first space.

Note

1. The authors are founders and designers of the P3C programme and Directors from 2009–2013. The programme was run in partnership with, and is certificated by The Tavistock Institute.

CHAPTER ONE

Potential space

Susan Rosina Whittle

We start this chapter by describing the importance of Winnicott's term "potential space" to our work. We explore the significance of play to creative consulting and change and the anxiety that can arise in developing both the true and the false self. The chapter ends with a brief summary of how these ideas influenced the design of The Tavistock Institute Practitioner Certificate in Consulting and Change (P3C), for those interested in the design of professional development programmes.

1.1 Potential space

Taking an experiential approach to change, we embrace Winnicott's concept of "potential space" to inform our thinking and the design of our professional development programmes.

Potential space "refers to an intermediate area of experiencing that lies between fantasy and reality" (Ogden, 1990, p. 203). Potential space originates in the "space between" infant and mother; in the "to and fro" (Winnicott, 1951, p. 55) of the mother as the infant learns what is "me" and what is "not me"; what is the internal world and what the external world. The infant's separation from mother both depends on and requires the child to move between the internal world of fantasy and external reality.

This move towards autonomy can be supported by the creation of a transitional object (Winnicott, 1953), such as a blanket, teddy bear, or part of the infant's own body, such as a thumb or hair. The power of the object to defend against the anxiety of separation comes from the object being unchanging, wholly controlled by the infant, and always available for comfort. Because it is a real object, with an independent reality, a transitional object offers the infant its first experience of a creative act and the exercise of control.

Potential space, as a zone of transition, is neither "me" nor "not me" but somewhere between, somewhere that play, that strange and creative mix of experience and imagination, occurs. Transitional zones, for Winnicott, are neutral spheres, free of the reality checks that are usually applied to actions and experiences, where play and illusion can flourish. Play, cultural life, and analytic activities are all examples of potential space, where objects are created. It is this creative energy, along with the fuzziness of boundaries (of what is me and not me; of what is real and what is imaginary; and of meaning) that gives potential space its appeal for professional development work.

At the same time, embracing the concept of potential space reminds us of the anxiety that can arise when faced with the threat of separation from those aspects of self we are attached to, or have learned to live with, and the routines that sustain them. Working in a potential space has the capacity to undermine the self I know and be destructive, as our containing routines are no longer available or sustained.

We need to keep this in mind in our programme design and ensure we create a "good object", a good enough holding environment to contain potentially destructive dynamics. By incorporating play, cultural, and analytic activities, can we offer a programme that affords participants "the opportunity … to move from dependence to autonomy" (Winnicott, 1951, p. 127). Can we encourage our adult learners to develop their own capacities to generate potential spaces for their own clients in their consulting work? We have brought these ideas to the design of this book.

1.2 Working with self

As resource-ful consultants, we have worked hard to know ourselves. We are in touch with and able to work with what Winnicott calls:

- the true self, whereby we are able to bring our experiences into our work spontaneously and authentically, and
- the false self, which exists in a preoccupied state of seeking to anticipate what is expected of us by others.

We know that the self develops in interaction with others, many others. So the true self does not refer to some Platonic essence that endures over time and place and is waiting to be discovered. The true self is who I am and how I behave when I am the agent of my own actions and not trying to behave how "I" think I should or to comply with the desires of others. In accessing the true self, we feel real in our work with clients and colleagues. This is not the same as being successful, valued, or admired. Being authentic helps us to address the difficult and sometimes unspoken issues that might otherwise remain buried under characteristics such as politeness and superficiality. These characteristics comprise the false self; whether our own or the false selves of our colleagues and our clients. The false self enables me to present myself in ways that hide how I really feel and avoid difficult encounters. This self helps me survive in a world that I fear might be risky or overwhelming, where I will be judged and found wanting; exposed as an imposter; lauded for my brilliance; derided for my imperfections; confronted in my certainty; or just ignored. In consulting, having access to a healthy false self is both a blessing and a curse. Authenticity has a price. Being able to contain those real, authentic thoughts and emotions that do not help meet my client development needs is essential. But knowing when, how and what to reveal of my true self, in service of the consulting task, is central to resourceful practice.

1.3 "Knowing me, knowing you"

Unlike the next line of Abba's hit song "Knowing me, knowing you, there is nothing we can do" (Andersson, Ulvaeus & Anderson, 1977), in this book we look at the ways consultants can choose and learn to influence what is revealed about themselves—to colleagues, clients, and to themselves. When do I feel real and spontaneous in my work? When do I feel complicit or "phoney", to use Winnicott's term? When am I carried along in the moment? Do I abandon myself to whatever ego dynamics (the behaviours arising from the triggering or mobilisation of different aspects of myself) prevail, only later to feel that I have mis-represented myself? These self dynamics shape presence and consulting practice in helpful and unhelpful ways, sometimes knowingly, sometimes unconsciously. Finding ways to understand how others encounter me helps me to make more informed choices about what I reveal about myself. The Johari window is a useful model for thinking about which aspects of myself I reveal, and to whom.

The model describes those aspects of myself:

- that are known to me and to others as the arena. This is an open space in which both you and I recognise the same aspects of myself. Maybe I am described as smart, sentimental, or a bit difficult to get to know; an expert in performance management or hopeless at public speaking.
- that I am unaware of but are known to others as my blind spot. A common dilemma for others is whether they make their knowledge available to me. Am I told that I my "jokes" offend my colleagues? Is my tendency to disregard the views of older women/HR professionals/

	Known to self	Not known to self
Known to others	**ARENA**	**BLIND SPOT**
Not known to others	**FAÇADE**	**UNKNOWN**

Figure 1.1 The Johari window (Luft & Ingham, 1955).

trade unions in my client organisations brought to my attention? Do I know I am good at my job or that I try to manipulate people?
- that are known to me but not known to others as the façade or hidden quadrant. How much do I reveal about myself to others? Do I have a façade, a professional self that hides my private self or am I the same at home and work? Maybe I never give much away about myself, wherever I am. There is also choice about what I reveal to others: that I am worried about working with them; that I could do this job much better on my own; that I'm glad I'm not leading; that I am looking for another job; that I have told others about our confidential conversations; that I really envy their success.
- that are not known to either myself or others as the unknown quadrant. This may be because there is very little knowledge available (perhaps at the beginning of a relationship, when opportunities for projection tend to be higher). Maybe some aspects of myself I hide unconsciously (that I dislike conflict or feel that I am better than most of my colleagues); or there is collusion between myself and others to make ourselves stupid and unknowing (Diamond, 2008). Awareness of the unknown or shadow self (Jung, 1951)[1] may be hidden both from others and from oneself because acknowledgement is embarrassing or shameful. It is "not me". (In Chapters Two and Three we explore some of these ideas in more detail).

Analytic Johari window analysis.

Quickly draw a Johari window.	Johari window	Known to self	Not known to self
In quadrant 1: Write some things about yourself that are known to you and to others. **In quadrant 2**: Write some things that you did not know until you were told by a colleague, client, or a friend. **In quadrant 3**: Write some things about yourself that are known to you but not to others.	Known to others	1. Open arena	2. Blind spot
In quadrant 4: Write some things that you have discovered about yourself that have surprised you and others.	Not known to others	3. Façade/ hidden	4. Unknown

The four quadrants or panes of the window can vary in size at different stages in our lives and with different people and places.[2]

- Looking at the four quadrants, which one(s) would you say typically describe your relationships with colleagues and with clients:
    - those where others know little about you or where they know a lot?
    - those where you feel you know yourself well or where you feel quite ignorant or unknowing about yourself?
- Think of two recent work assignments and your relationships with the people involved. Compare them using the Johari window. In which assignment would you say:
    - You revealed more about yourself to others?
    - You chose not to reveal something about yourself to others?
    - You discovered something previously unknown about yourself?
- What do you think might explain the differences?

It's likely that I have put in place routines, to manage how I bring myself to my work. These help to defend me against the unexpected and the uninvited pulls on what I reveal and what I choose to remain hidden. But these same routines can start to feel like an iron cage from which I seem unable to escape. It is "as if there is an inner figure opposed to myself [which] is the source of action". (Symington, 1993, p. 115).

> Abigail is an accomplished and well respected organisation change consultant and academic. She has a strong and diverse network of fellow practitioners, some of whom she knows very well, but few know much about her. She is frequently asked for advice and references, or about new developments and invited to contribute to conferences and events. But she finds herself avoiding opportunities to socialise. With her domestic and family responsibilities, Abigail says it is time "not well spent". She also knows that, without the routine of work to talk about, she will feel uncomfortable and leave social events as soon as possible, thinking "It's not for me".

This inner figure, or inner voice, develops in infancy and with appropriate care-giving is able to defend me against feelings of being overwhelmed or unsafe when I face risky and challenging experiences. But in the absence of good enough (Winnicott, 1957) and attuned care-giving, the child's inner world can develop with few or no resources to draw on, leaving a depleted inner world, with no reassuring voices, or one occupied by an alarmingly grandiose voice. Rather than a resource offering a rich and accessible sense of myself, the inner world is inhabited by a fearful, indifferent, or querulous figure. Because this inner figure may lie hidden behind a well-crafted and carefully constructed professional persona, acting out may provide one of the few clues to its existence.

> ### Box 1.1 Acting out
>
> When a child loses a pet, an adult experiences a difficult divorce, or when an older man is made redundant, the feelings evoked may be acted out rather than spoken: anger, loss of appetite, loss of confidence, withdrawal, excessive activity, daydreaming, or avoidance of others (Bowlby, 1980).
>
> When I behave in ways that give expression to thoughts and emotions that I cannot bring myself to acknowledge consciously, I am acting out.
>
> I act out those things that I cannot voice perhaps because:
>
> - I don't know how to express my thoughts or feelings, like a child having a tantrum.
> - Unconsciously, I fear the consequences for me or others of revealing my thoughts or feelings. Will I be rejected, ridiculed, or have to act on what I say?
> - I find the shame of my thoughts or feelings unbearable. Maybe they signal disloyalty, betrayal, inappropriate emotions, or some characteristic that I consider to be "not me".
>
> Where thoughts and feelings persist in their unacknowledged form, acting out can develop into compulsion, which brings further difficulties.
>
> Jake's diary is always full. He likes it that way. He couldn't bear to have time on his hands, not knowing what he should be doing. Sometimes he can't keep commitments because he has an overfull diary. People tell him he's ambitious, but he's just trying to work hard and do his best, as everyone should. He has decided to enrol on another residential development programme. His coach tells him that's what he needs. He didn't manage to complete the last one due to clashes with his work schedule. He knows he might have to make sacrifices whilst on the programme, not socialising during breaks or in the evening because he will have to make work calls. Maybe there is a quicker distance learning programme he could do that fits into his routine?

It's not easy to take off the "shoddy armour" (Kohut, 1984) that protects me from anxieties evoked by those aspects of me that I consider too vulnerable to reveal or those I fear are too destructive to let loose on my colleagues and clients. The challenge is to find ways to;

- help reveal the inner voice and dysfunctional routines of self management which hinder me from learning new ways of thinking and behaving
- take up opportunities to change those routines as appropriate
- provide sufficient containment to support practical experimentation through play.

1.4 Play

Play is found in many species. Through play, young mammals learn to hunt or live together without the risks they usually incur. In humans, play does not end with adulthood but continues in games, sports, contests of all sorts, jokes and pranks, and hobbies. The fact that I can say "I'm only playing at it" licences very many people to paint, join a choir, or play football. This "not-really-me-but-I'm-having-a-go" frame of mind is a tentative form of reinvention of the self and it's happening in a safe space; somewhere I won't feel judged for not being very proficient because "it's only a hobby" or a "bit of fun".

Because of the indeterminate relationship between what is real and what is imagined, "playing is inherently exciting and precarious" (Winnicott, 1951, p. 61). The idea of playing depends on maintaining the distinction between a symbol and what is symbolised, or objects and the meanings afforded to them. Whilst an adult sees a saucepan as something to cook in, to a child it is a drum or a hat. A cardboard box is a car or a den. Play takes the real object (the pan or cardboard box) and affords it new meaning (a drum, a car). Play does not lose touch with reality, but creatively reinvents it.

> For young children, the sofa can easily become a boat, making its way through the dangerous waters of the lounge, full of sharks and other unthinkable terrors, towards the island haven that is Dad's armchair. I join in and find myself shrieking with fright when pushed into the water!

The magic of play as a potential space is easily disrupted. If children are told "Don't be silly!", "Jumping around like that is dangerous", "You will damage the chair", the spell is broken. Potential space ceases to exist when that indeterminate relationship between the real and the imagined is suddenly clarified. The presence of a non-player, of someone not joining-in, or a judgemental authority figure can kill the potential in the space. This is why presence is always an intervention, needing design and management.

1.5 How could we design play into a professional development programme?

Games are integral to the design of many development programmes. The simulation or role-play has game-like qualities in which we are invited to take up the roles we are given in a pre-planned scenario. Play tends to be a more open space, with rules and roles emerging in the moment and often contested. Yes, play can become institutionalised over time. Playing at something (such as shops or fighting) gradually takes on more game-like qualities until it is judged inappropriate to continue referring to games such as rugby, cricket, or baseball as play.

Games are a particular form of play, where everyday reality is temporarily suspended and unusual behaviours, such as shouting, grabbing, dressing strangely, and competing are permitted. Games are usually designed before participation begins, such that a priori rules and indicators of right and wrong, winners and losers, prescribe who does what and how to do it. Games, like play, also evoke emotion and creativity as contestants experiment with and subvert rules and roles in order to win (Gergen & Kaye, 1992).

Games can be serious, as can play. Serious play "is not necessarily fun. It can entail pain and conflict when people are challenged to act outside their normal behavioural repertoires, and to challenge their normal assumptions" (Beech et al., 2004, p. 1329).

We design play into professional development for consultants and change agents to equip them to better meet the turbulence we now encounter in the world of work, where preset interventions and repeat practices fall short. If we can create an environment that is "good enough" (Winnicott, 1957) to support this learning and development, our programme participants can rediscover, through play, that they can bring creativity and imagination to their work and to themselves.

> **Forbes News Flash**—innovation, growth and development cannot occur by pretending we live in a world that has long since passed us by.
>
> Leading in the 21st Century affords no safe haven for 20th Century thinkers … Smart leaders simply don't waste precious resources on refining initiatives—they invest in re-imagination efforts. Leaders would be well served to apply re-imagination to all aspects of their business, but particularly with regard to constantly reimagining how they lead … Many leaders struggle to remain current, much less find a way to move ahead of the curve. Here's the thing—if leaders are stuck in the past, their organizations will be forced to travel a very rough road to the future. (http://www.forbes.com/sites/mikemyatt/2013/03/07/10-things-every-leader-should-challenge/)

Our approach is always experiential (Kolb, 1984). Some consider that playing is always integral to experiential learning: "play has been central to the practice of experiential learning; be it games, role plays, outdoor adventure training or 'playing' with ideas in the creative process" (Kolb & Kolb, 2010, p. 27). However, we consider role-plays and simulations are better described as games. Games tend to evoke compliance with decisions already taken by those in authority and evoke little in the way of creativity. Winnicott described creativity as "the retention throughout life" of the "ability to create the world" (Winnicott, 1986, p. 40). This requires that we are confident both in arriving at our own interpretations of our experiences and in taking action informed by them, rather than depending on others to make sense of what is going on and telling us what to do.

Play, as a potential space, "opens up possibilities for individuals to become intrinsically motivated to define for themselves what to learn, how to deal with change, and ultimately reinventing themselves within the safety of the space" (Kolb & Kolb, 2010, p. 27).

1.6 The P3C programme design

For The Tavistock Institute Practitioner Certificate in Consulting and Change Programme (P3C), we decided to introduce co-construction into the design, to encourage participants to take up their own agency. To some extent, this is always an aspect of experiential programmes, in that what happens in time bounded sessions is necessarily emergent. We took this further, not only inviting participants to co-create designs for sessions but responding in the moment to their requests and demands to reinvent the schedule, tasks, and roles. This meant we had to consider our own practice as programme directors. When every moment is potentially a "new moment", in which each individual can ask "what do I want for myself." (Janette Rainwater, quoted in Giddens, 1991), we were mind-ful that no-one is immune from ongoing choices about how to be present at work. The P3C programme would also offer a potential space for directors to work on our own dysfunctional routines! We knew we needed to avoid falling into what worked in the past. We would help participants step out of their routines by stepping out of our own. This meant:

- keeping in mind task, territory, and time
- containment of the pull to over-design

- containment of the anxiety that working in this way might not work
- real time feedback between directors to catch sight of ourselves.

From many years of educational and coaching work, we were also acutely aware that our consultant participants would bring their considerable experiences of other development programs with them. We would be working with the dynamics of their own learning histories before we even started (Sama, 2009). We would need to address the paradox of the "take no notice of this notice" message and design the program:

1. to enable participants to take up their own agency and engage with both their experiences on the program and of each other spontaneously and authentically
   - through co-construction
   - through authorisation, own decision-making, and optional participation
   - through explicit contracting
   - through group sanctions
   - through spending time on the back story—understanding and calling actions to account.

2. to overcome any disconnects between saying and doing:
   - by working with showing as well as telling
   - by demonstrating how to work
   - by using the self as instrument to intervene during the program to design, challenge, apologise, not know, be confused, lead, hold etc.

The programme began with these specifications in mind. The first session invited participants to talk about themselves and their practice using an object or artefact they have brought with them. (More details on the ethos and design of the programme can be found in Appendix one to this book.) As people can enrol on experiential programmes and yet still expect to be taught, a contracting session followed immediately. In this session, to make the design specification of the programme more accessible and contain anxieties, the P3C programme was described explicitly as offering a potential space to work on professional practice needs by:

- Using here and now experiences
- Experimenting, hypothesising, theorising
- Crafting, collaborating, and co-creating interventions
- Addressing perpetual preoccupations
- Developing self as instrument.

They are shown in Figure 1.2. These aspects of the design are like balls that programme directors need to attend to and keep in the air all at the same time. They are also essential to resource-ful consulting and comprise elements of the competence profile against which P3C participants are assessed. (See Chapter Seven.) This is the context we worked to create on the programme—with participants having several simultaneous tasks, designed to decentre their focus on learning about their development and replace it with developing by doing.

10   RESOURCE-FUL CONSULTING

©Susan Rosina Whittle

Figure 1.2 P3C a potential space to …

In 2009 we had published *Mind-ful Consulting* (Whittle & Izod, 2009) and this collection of stories of consulting practice became one of our core texts. Over four years of the P3C programme, we became more and more aware of the significance of presence as an intervention and the power of identity and authority to shape presence. The next two chapters explore the dynamics, the trips and traps, associated with these aspects of ourselves as we work in consulting and change.

Notes

1. http://changingminds.org/explanations/identity/jung_archetypes.htm
2. Follow this link http://www.businessballs.com/johariwindowmodel.htm for information about using the Johari Window model and how the four quadrants or panes of the window can vary in size.

CHAPTER TWO

Identity

Karen Izod

Rather like airline advice to fit our own oxygen masks before helping others, attending to "who I am" and "who I am not" at any one time is an effective way to think about the rationale behind the idea of developing ourselves as instruments as we engage with colleagues and clients to effect change.

In this section you will find:

- Some ideas about inhabiting our identities—what this means
- Why working with identity is so central to our approach to professional development
- Accounts from organisational consulting and change practitioners as to how identity makes itself felt in our practice, together with theories to help you think about identities in relation to different consulting challenges.

The section is interspersed with analytic activities to help you notice and work on your own identity preoccupations.

2.1 Inhabiting identities—what this means

Whenever I am invited to create a brief profile for a client, or upload new information on a social media site, then I am instantly posed with a challenge as to how I describe myself, and which aspects of myself I choose to convey. I need to be comfortable enough in my skin to take up the tasks of consulting to and managing change: doing, thinking, knowing, changing, evaluating. Unlike Jamie Oliver and "The Naked Chef" (1999), I'm not going to refer to myself as "naked", but nor do I want to be so bundled up in accumulations of identities that I can't be touched by my experiences. I wear my identities on my face, in my clothes, in the way I relate to others.

As a consultant, I think about how I can make best use of who I am, in this moment, with this client. I find myself paying attention to who I bring with me, with the intention, at least, of being sufficiently receptive and agile in my thoughts, feelings, and behaviours. I inhabit identities, and in the main I can make choices about which identities I want to live in, and how long they are helpful to me, before I decide it is time to slough them off, or modify them in some way. I also own my identities and, as with any kind of ownership, they afford benefits and privileges, and also come at a cost. I may own an identity that requires taking on responsibilities: in the eyes of the law being an adult rather than a child for instance. Or I may own an identity that constantly lends itself to being overlooked, or bypassed, as with a junior member of a team, or a non-native language speaker.

It can be hard to escape from some identities once they are taken on. It is not that easy to extricate oneself from a professional identity developed through training, or the commitment of being married. Similarly it is hard to escape from the way others impose their view of my identity, relating to me in ways that feel alien, the not-me. Identity is ever present as a feature of how I engage with my clients. Noticing who I am, and also, who I am not, is a key ingredient in how I make sense of my work experiences.

2.2 What is identity?

When I think of my identity, I think of a combination of characteristics about me; the way I think, feel, and behave, together with those individual qualities and attributes that blend into something that is recognisably and uniquely me. This recognisability is usually seen as sufficient to offer coherence in my life. Even when I find that I am behaving "out of sorts", there is sufficient that is recognisable to offer continuity, such that my sense of self is not disturbed to a point where I lose my capacity to function.

My self can be thought of as the composite of multiple characteristics (social, physical, emotional, and psychological) which coexist at any one time. This is about our existence: taking up a place in the world, as thinking, feeling individuals, (Giddens, 1991) and is the basis for our subjectivity. As a mental structure, my self provides a largely unconscious, reflexive representation of who I am, in relation to others. Our view is that the self is constantly in flux, influenced by interactions with others in the social world, and therefore capable of change. Some aspects of our selves become deeply rooted. We identify strongly with characteristics which we have encountered through the senses in the touch, sounds, sights, and smells internalised in early infancy from repeated interactions with attachment figures (Rustin, 1991). These form identity signifiers, clues as to who we are, and the way that we structure and make sense of the world.[1] These multiple signifiers reveal different aspects of the self which may be in tension with one another. Take for example the consultant who is ambitious for success, but comes up against the part of herself that expects to be quickly gratified and resists putting in the hours to build expertise and knowledge.

Identity signifiers are words I can use to describe myself: woman, middle-aged, short, white, English. These are descriptors of characteristics I don't have that much choice about: they are given characteristics that relate to living and being in a place and in a time, and are therefore open to different cultural meanings (Ibarra & Petriglieri, 2007). They are apparent to anyone I meet, and for the most part unchangeable. Yet how important they are to my sense of self will depend on the values that I place on these characteristics, and how much they are present in the minds of others. All too easily they can be clustered as stereotypes and precede me as signifiers which are hard to get beyond, and push other aspects of my identity into the shadows—humorous, gregarious, a consultant! Although I don't have a choice about owning these given characteristics, I do have a choice about how I relate to them.

I also have identity signifiers that I can determine for myself: how my interests crystallise into activities and careers, my lifestyle preferences and responsibilities, where I live, who I make intimate relationships and friendships with, and how I like to spend my time. These may be observable to my work colleagues and clients, but I can make a judgement call as to how much I am comfortable to reveal, and what it is helpful for my client to know. Is it helpful, for instance, to let my clients know what my political affiliations might be, or whether or not I am a parent? There are no rules. As I switch between professional tasks, coaching, running workshops, working with a team in conflict, then so I have to work with my awareness as to what these signifiers might mean in my working context, and how my clients might identify with or feel at odds with what I reveal.

Identities are also attributed to us by others who ascribe meaning to how we behave, and what our identities evoke for them. Recognising and relating to facial expressions, bodily gestures, and use of language all depend on contextual and cultural clues, and how we choose to interpret them. Adolescents in particular have a heightened sensitivity to minute differentiations in clothes, hairstyles, musical tastes, as they work out who they are in relation to others. Yet these differentiators are often immaterial to others. An elderly person might feel quite threatened as they walk towards a group of teenagers, and the teenagers themselves might be quite shocked to learn that they are seen in this way. We tend to place emotional values on these different identity signifiers so that we admire some, and denigrate others, and this forms a basis for stereotyping and prejudice.

Here are some of the identities that consultants we work with chose to introduce themselves professionally.

Box 2.1 Introducing ourselves
I work with small businesses, I offer training to the sector
I have a fairly conventional HR role, I'm mainly working on reducing the workforce
I'm the head of faculty, I don't do much teaching, I have to restructure things
I'm in a transition from being an internal consultant in a big firm, to setting up my own practice
I'm in a knowledge transfer role, I have to bring a business mind to a public enterprise
I'm French, I live in Switzerland, I'm married to an Australian
I have two grown up sons
I'm very knowledgeable about the public sector
I'm very active and keep myself fit
I'm facing redundancy
I know I'm vulnerable but I try not to show it
I read very widely across different genres

In the main, these identities make use of an imagined "other", the "not-me". To refer to myself as having a business mind brings into being a "not-me", the person with the artistic mind, for instance. Describing myself as working in a conventional role brings into being the "not-me" of the non-conventional, or the innovative. This idea of the other is at work in our minds as we choose what we want to reveal about ourselves, and starts to differentiate us to make us seem more like x and less like y. When x and y are individuals or groups within our client systems, we start to choose with whom we want to align ourselves, and with whom we want to keep a distance.

2.3 Why working with identity is so central to our approach to professional development

Two things are important for us here: allowing myself sufficient space to work, and to use my identities as interpretative structures.

1. To allow myself sufficient space to work, is to not get caught up in identities which either belong to the past, or which have never served me well. I need to be aware of my identities to be able to access real and symbolic resources—stories, artefacts, places, cultures, knowledge that will help me to bring my authentic self to the client.

   Here are two examples of how consultants are tripped up and trapped in their identities.

   > Vincenze was a logistics manager in the food industry before moving into consultancy specialising in supply chain processes. He named his identity signifiers as efficiency, economy, and outcome orientation, which combined with his role as manager meant that he was in a good position for influencing how things were done.
   >
   > As a consultant Vincenze easily brings these signifiers from the past into his existing role, where he can fall into the trap of making up the gaps he perceives in his client's operational systems, rather than thinking about how they can be addressed. As a skilled manager, he finds it difficult to avoid stepping into management tasks, and making sure they are done. Vincenze is aware that filling the gaps diminishes his capacity to bring his consultant identity to the client and he loses opportunities to work with a broader perspective and range of people. He hears terms like interim manager or project manager being applied to him.

   > The history of Melanie's organisational change role in a large, publicly funded body situates her outside the main directorate, in a semi-independent business unit. This structural dislocation means that she is attributed with words like "loose cannon", "a bit of a maverick", as if she is unaccountable in the same way as her peers. Melanie rather likes this image of herself, which she uses to her advantage to take initiatives across the organisation. On the other hand, she gets tripped up by her identity, specifically when questions of authorisation and credibility for her work come to the fore. She can find herself being left out of important discussions.

   Both Melanie and Vincenze are holding on to identities that have served them well in the past, or to which they have a strong emotional investment. But now, in their present roles, these identities can catch them out. When I am accessing an identity that can trip me up in the present, or trap me in the past, then I run the risk that it is not fit for this purpose, now. Of course, we can't always tell what is fit for purpose, and for Melanie, being able to access both the maverick and the authorised can be helpful. It is a question of building up our awareness that this is what we are doing so as not to be taken by surprise.

2. Our identities provide us with "interpretative structures" (Marris, 1982) through which we can begin to attribute meaning, and work with intention. In a sense, they authorise us to think and behave as we do. The foundations for these interpretative structures are formed in unique early relationships, through which we can have our thoughts and feelings confirmed

as valid (see recognition section below). Such a structure enables us to classify and predict: What is this situation? Do I recognise it? What might I see happen next? It gives us data against which I can measure my experiences and test them for accuracy. If I can make sense of my feelings and intentions then I stand a chance of finding purpose, and giving direction to my actions. When we talk of someone being "grounded" in their work, then this will usually mean that we encounter them as in touch with their physical and emotional world, and that their actions connect in a sufficiently understandable way. When we find ourselves saying "I didn't see that coming", or when we are unable to make links for our clients between what their experiences and our intervention suggestions, then we know that there is a disconnection, that meaning is temporarily unavailable, or yet to be found.

Here are some examples of how our identities operate as interpretive structures influencing the way we understand and make sense of our experiences:

Box 2.2 Identities and meaning-making

Identity	?????
Psychotherapist	It's easy for me to see symptoms, to feel that someone is vulnerable, and for me to see them as less than resilient. I have to catch myself when I think like this.
Youngest child	I tend to think that everyone knows more than I do. It makes it hard to offer my thinking because I imagine it is going to be shot down.
Social worker/consultant	My social work clients think I am very academic. My academic clients think I am very practical.
UK consultant working in France	I don't really get the cultural nuances yet, I feel my boss is very distant, and I tend to feel I can't meet her expectations.

Analytic What examples do you encounter?

Try filling in this grid from the different identities you inhabit.	
My identity	????

2.4 Accounts from organisational development and change practitioners as to how identity makes itself felt in our practice

We have found that three aspects of identity interact to support the way we make meaning, and to inform our professional practice:

RECOGNITION: How I come to know "who I am" and "what I am"?
REGULATION: Which of my emotions do I need to manage, and how can I do that?
REVELATION: Which of my identities are revealed more easily/less easily?

We will explore these dynamic aspects of identity and the preoccupations they foster, through the accounts of practitioners.

2.4.1 Recognition—how I come to know "who I am" and "what I am"

> My boss can only relate to me as his "next in command". It's a military image and implies subordination. It's not a language that I would choose for myself, and doesn't fit with my own image as someone who is a specialist and creative, with a job in my own right. Yet I know that it influences the way that I think about myself in this company, and I struggle to hold on to my competent side. It's a vicious cycle.
> *Ekke: Swedish Marketing Manager.*

Ekke's energy is being diverted into "identity" work here, as he attempts to maintain a sense of who he is in this situation. He is trapped in the identity that his boss attributes to him and he faces a challenge of how to actively influence his perceptions so that they are more in line with his own. Otherwise he risks a passive acceptance which over time solidifies as a reputation.

> Aadit is a development manager for a small charity concerned with mental health. It is one of a number of similar charities who in partnership are collaborating with a central government department to consider policy implications in practice. He describes how "as my organisation has got bigger and attracts more money, then so I'm no longer seen as someone to be invited in, as collaborative. I'm seen as someone who calls the shots, and this isn't a project for big players it's a project for small players who need to have a voice. Now I find that I haven't got a voice—I'm being squeezed out".

Aadit is being tripped up as he negotiates the shifting ground of his organisation, and how this is seen by others, where the perceived power of his organisation is now working against him. His identity, as a peer in this partnership, is being threatened and he is facing the loss of a known identity, representing a known organisation, and with it, his repertoire of relating to his colleagues.

Sayings like "I don't feel like myself today", or "I'm besides myself with anger" indicate that we have a sense of a "me", and what it feels like to be me. At some point in our social and emotional development we have reached a position of knowing that I am separate and different, and what goes on in my mind and the way that I think and feel about things is unique to me, and therefore different from you. Children can sometimes find this a scary notion, particularly if it leads to a feeling of isolation from others, or a sense that their experiences can't be understood.

18   RESOURCE-FUL CONSULTING

So how do we come to inhabit our minds and bodies in a way which says—this is me, and conversely, this is not me. Our understanding of how we develop comes from a "relational" psychoanalytic tradition (Clarke, Hahn & Hoggett, 2009), which sees individual development as embedded in a social world and context, and based on interactions with others. From our earliest moments in life, we are involved in minute interactions with others, which are repeated over time. Patterns of interactions with mothers, fathers, and others who care for us register in our experiences of our bodies, the way our brain develops, the emotions that are then available to us, and are central to how we see ourselves.

Figure 2.1 Mirroring.

IDENTITY   19

2.4.1a Mirroring

Mirroring is a process that occurs when a parent visibly responds to an infant, picking up their mood, and ideally attuning themselves to it, in such a way that the infant catches a glimpse of themselves. This isn't necessarily a straightforward process. Parents have many moods and responses of their own, and the emotional pictures that they send back may communicate many different impressions for the infant to register. But what the mother or father's face portrays is related to "what they see in the baby, and what the baby sees is itself" (Winnicott, 1967, in Rustin, 1991, p. 186). This is the way that patterns develop such that the infant comes to gain an image and a sense of "who I am". I become familiar to myself, and to others: I can "recognise" myself.

I talked about identity signifiers as being words that I use to describe my characteristics, and these will derive from these early patterns of interaction, so words like shy, outgoing, observer, always on the go, worrier, laid-back, and so on, cluster to form patterns in our behaviour. (The extent to which we may be aware of these, or blind to them will be discussed in Chapter Three). But to the extent that we are aware of these characteristics, then so we can have an awareness of what sits recognisably with me, and what doesn't.

Analytic   Being recognised and helping myself be recognisable.

> **Think again of the situation you described in the previous analytic and consider the following questions:**
>
> - Do I feel recognised by my client?
> - Do I recognise this picture of myself that is mirrored back to me in my work—is it accurate or distorted? How can I test this out?
> - Where don't I feel recognised, what am I saying/doing?
> - What do I need to retrieve or modify about my identity for this encounter to be more authentic?

2.4.2   Regulation—which of my emotions do I need to manage and how can I do that?

> Everything that I do, with my new identity as an independent consultant, raises questions for me about how I behave. I've been used to working with very clear boundaries in my previous organisation, only having to manage the time when I am face to face with my client, for instance. Now I have to manage all the in-between times, I am constantly thinking about my clients, I feel constantly available to them. I know I have to find new ways of relating from this identity., so as to not feel so overwhelmed. *Noele: freelance learning and development specialist.*

> In my first meeting with the client, I was constantly thinking about my relationship with my co-consultant. I felt very ineffectual in relation to him, I couldn't shake off the feeling that I had to prove myself. It meant that I didn't actually hear what the client was saying, and then when I needed to summarise and make a proposal, I was lost. *Clive: relationship manager, niche consultancy firm.*

Both of these accounts illustrate some kind of displacement of who I am, and what I bring, that disturbs my everyday sense of self. In Noele's situation, she cannot fall back on her usual repertoire as to how she spends her time and makes herself available to her clients; it is as if her former identity and the way she could think in that role cannot transfer to the present and is lost to her. For Clive, something else has come into the picture that is claiming his attention; his usually competent self has been displaced in this time and this place, and he has to try to find some distance between the powerful emotions that are influencing him, and the management of the session with the client that he is there to do.

The term "regulation" comes from the work by Fonagy, Gergely, Jurist & Target, 2004, on "regulation of affect": that is, how can I manage my feelings and emotions and how can I make use of others to relieve or accentuate that? The patterns of interaction over time that I mentioned earlier (recognition above) form our capacity to regulate how much sleep, food, comfort, I need, and to negotiate with others for that.

The same applies to our emotional range: finding the level of how much joy, distress, confusion, I can manage at any one time involves me in ways of relating to others, such that they can help to contain and balance my emotions for me, or bolster me up in a way that I don't have to do for myself. They form patterns of relating.

This is an analysis of a contracting meeting I had with a new client, and some of the emotions that I was aware of at the time.

Box 2.3 Emotions generated/regulated in contracting

	Emotions that helped me keep on track	Emotions that derailed me for the moment
Excited at the prospect of working with this client		✓
Daunted by what was being asked of me	✓	
Wondering if I am the right person to do the work		✓
Angry about the client's situation even when they didn't seem to be	✓	✓

My awareness of these emotions and their impact on me suggest that I need to find a way to not be taken over by my inner world, making sure that excitement at the work doesn't take me off into flights of fantasy about my own importance, nor that I am unrealistic about what the work will involve. At the same time, my emotional register is an important source of data about what might be happening in this exchange. The anger that I was in touch with in myself, but which didn't seem to have been expressed by the client, is something that I have to sit with for a while, until I have a sense of what it might be about, and where it might be coming from.

Analytic Emotions generated/regulated in contracting.

> Try filling out the box above for a number of your consulting assignments or change projects.
>
> What are the emotions that you encounter? Do they help you to keep on task or derail you in some way?

2.4.2a Containment

We make the assumption that we can constantly remake, or redefine the distance between our inner and outer lives, and that key to this process is the concept of containment.

Containment is a means of regulating (or being helped to regulate) my emotions in the face of anxiety and frustration, and is often necessary when there is some kind of threat or dislocation to our identity, getting in the way of ordinarily good functioning (Grueneisen & Izod, 2009).

We can do this for ourselves through:

- Ritual—I'm going to tidy up the cupboard/have a cup of coffee/take the dog for a walk, allow myself to feel badly done by before I write this report.
- External stimuli—I can work better with the television on.
- Making use of a transitional object, (see Chapter One) something that holds an element of the anxiety, but can modify it—this might be through working in the same room with trusted colleagues, using relied upon methods, and accessing art forms such as reading poetry, drawing a picture, making use of a metaphor.

Containment can also be encountered through others:

- Being involved in interaction with others in which our thoughts and feelings can be seen as valid, and recognised as belonging to us. This gives us the space to gain distance from the experience and to reflect, broadening the range of options available to us.

Different working environments and organisational cultures can help or hinder this capacity to be contained and access a thinking space: think for instance of envious dynamics where your views might be constantly belittled, or power dynamics where only one view can be allowed.

In our professional development programmes we make use of a metaphor of a harbour—a safe place, in sight of, but protected from the winds and fortunes. Working with this can offer a "time out" stopping proceedings to allow for fresh thinking, and opportunity to get back in touch with my identity and competence.

2.4.3 Revelation—Which of my identities are revealed more easily/less easily?

> Silvia designs and facilitates large-scale employee engagement interventions in a knowledge/information systems organisation. She is very visible in this role, but feels that her identities don't serve her well, and that she constantly has to prove herself. Relatively new to the company she hasn't come up through the ranks, and has a non-technical background which she feels disadvantages her in spite of her expert knowledge on human process.

22 RESOURCE-FUL CONSULTING

Silvia faces a dilemma as to how she is seen in her company. It is a given that she is new, and from a non-technical background. These are identities which she owns, even if she wishes it otherwise in this specific organisational culture. The difficulty is the extent to which these identities are in the foreground—and with them various associated feelings of being seen as naïve, inexperienced, lacking knowledge. Certainly these feelings are not unusual in the early days of an appointment, but for the moment she has lost sight of whatever skills and experience her employers saw in her when they took her on for the job of human resource specialist. Her identities are her weaknesses rather than her strengths.

Attributed identities can be powerful, and in Silvia's situation her newness and non-technical background have gained prominence in her mind, influencing her perception of who she is. How does this happen? The concept of projection is one way of understanding this.

2.4.3a Projection and transference

Projection is a defence mechanism which operates unconsciously to protect us from painful and unwanted emotions. Rather like a film projector casting its beam onto a screen, we can project

Figure 2.2 Projection.

these feelings onto, and into other people. Successful projections—those that we can lodge with another person, limit the range of emotions that we are exposed to, usually resulting in us being able to cope with otherwise intolerable feelings. In that sense, we lose a part of ourselves, and make the unwanted part a "not-me". In Sylvia's case, we could hypothesise that other people in her organisation feel inexperienced and lack knowledge that they need, but that in order to function on an everyday level, it becomes easier to project those feelings onto her.

But people aren't blank screens, we ourselves attract projections. We need a sensitivity for the feelings that others cast off. Without that magnet type quality, then projections fall flat. Sylvia as the new human resource specialist, is a prime candidate to project these feelings onto since her identities are already being challenged by her newness and her experience of not being recognised in her more successful identities.

As the recipient of projections, then I may be acutely aware of my feelings being activated according to what I am picking up—helplessness, vulnerability, agitation, over-confidence, cockiness. In this situation I have a sense of being "not-quite-me". This acts as an alert that something is going on, so that I can start to think about it, and understand what it might be about. But on occasions, the projection may be very close to home, may fit with me to a degree that I internalise it and start to behave as if it "is" me. Somebody else's "not wanted me", becomes "me", and I am being mobilised to take on emotions for someone else. This in turn influences the way that I behave.

It helps to notice what emotions we are particularly prone to picking up from others. Some, like restlessness or irritation don't necessarily have to be projections but belong to body language and mood. If I am sitting next to someone who is giving off waves of irritation then I can easily become irritated myself. Laughter, fun, and excitement is infectious. Other emotions like feeling blame, shame, and listless are more personalised.

Analytic Noticing emotional tendencies.

Think of a recent group that you were involved in and note:	
Emotions that I felt in the encounter	"My sense of whether this was "me", or "not quite me"

Build up a picture from a range of meetings or discussions to see if there are any emotions that repeat, and that might indicate your tendency to be mobilised by others.

Transference is an additional unconscious process that influences my sense of what is "me" and "not me", and describes the way in which I can relate to another person as if they are someone else from another time and place. Family figures, figures of love and affection, hate and rejection, authority figures, wish-fulfilment figures are easily evoked in situations which approximate to their origins. In our roles as directors of P3C and shadow consultants, then it is easy for us to attract feelings that belong to others, such as head teachers, line managers, parents, and to find ourselves being related to in those types of role. This is where the potential for acting on these "as if" relationships is high (see Chapter One). Small groups easily stir up transferences from earlier family life, with parents and siblings. Much as with projections, then I can also find myself relating to these transferences "as if" they are me, and my identities as a mother, or as a little sister can be evoked and come to the fore.

Richard is in this kind of situation in his project team.

> I realise that I am in a process of change myself, taking up this responsibility for change within my new marketing directorship. So far, I haven't found a way to influence things from this role. I continually feel disoriented, and can't hold on to what my own views are, let alone think about how to give direction to the change initiative. *Richard: marketing director, Pharmaceuticals.*

Further discussion with Richard, and the way that his colleagues related to him in our P3C "learning out loud" groups, indicated just how easy it was to relate to Richard as a bossy big brother, expecting him to organise them and to take responsibility. We could hypothesise that this was a combination of a projection, needing him to take the lead, so that others didn't have to face not knowing what to do, and for some group members, a transference towards him from familial roles. Richard is challenged with how to construct identities for himself that enable him to step out from behind these roles, and find a mode of relating that enables him to direct the work in a more mindful way.

Analytic Transferred emotion and role.

See if you can notice situations where you step into modes of relating that are being transferred from other people and other times. Roles such as joker, peacemaker, tension breaker, ignoramus, nurturer are easily evoked and transferred from earlier relationships.

2.5 Summary

These are the dynamics of identity that we have been exploring:

RECOGNITION: How I come to know "who I am" and "what I am"?
REGULATION: Which of my emotions do I need to manage, and how can I do that?
REVELATION: Which of my identities are revealed more easily/less easily?

Practitioner narratives illustrate how these different dynamics of identity are interrelated, and self-reinforcing. They serve as resources to access in our consulting work, either knowingly or by default, in the roles that we take up, and as we craft a presence for ourselves in the way that we intervene with our client organisations.

Chapter Three looks at the dynamic properties of presence.

Note

1. For helpful description of Lacan's work on identity see http://www.iep.utm.edu/lacweb/#SH4a last accessed 23 May 2013.

CHAPTER THREE

Presence

Susan Rosina Whittle

In this chapter we turn to presence and why it matters. After describing three powerful authority dynamics that shape presence (confidence, competition, and control), we consider intended and unintended presence, and the links between presence and transference. Throughout this section, we invite you to explore what you know about your own presence and whether you are preoccupied with confidence, competition, and/or control.

3.1 Presence matters

Most of us have a day when we work with colleagues, run an event, or encounter a client and think:

"I could have handled that better".
"I let myself down".
"Who does he think he is? It was my meeting".
"I had an off day. They didn't see the best of me".
"I lost it there. What happened?"

Sometimes, these experiences start to repeat. I begin to notice people responding to me in ways that are surprising or puzzling, perhaps not responding at all. I can identify situations that are "difficult", perhaps where I lose my confidence and talk too much or too little or where I end up taking the minutes rather than leading the discussion. In these situations, I am becoming aware of a problem with my presence. Perhaps there is a mismatch between how others encounter me and how I think of myself. Maybe I behave as I always do, as others expect me to: speaking out or playing the fool; easily derailed and flustered; always the good cop and never the bad cop.

In Chapter Two, we looked at how identity shapes professional practice through the dynamics of recognition, regulation, and revelation. In that chapter, the focus was on the internal world and how I develop a sense of myself overtime, giving some recognisable coherence to who I am. Identity can also be thrust upon me uninvited, by others. So it is with presence. Others can be complicit in shaping my presence in ways that are unhelpful to my practice, my development and my client's development. To influence and maybe change how others encounter me, I need to own my presence.

But becoming aware of how colleagues and clients experience my presence is not easy. Here are comments from consultants I have worked with about how they encounter their colleagues.

Box 3.1 Encountering colleagues

I can't stand it. I bet she tells another one of her tear jerking stories and we are all expected to listen and be moved.

He hogs the space all the time. I don't want to listen to him.

He has to be the last to speak, as if he's special or speaking on behalf of us all.

She hides behind complicated language. Maybe she doesn't have much to say?

She's not my mother.

I don't know why he assumes he has to be in charge. He cannot take up any other role in this group. I am fed up of working with him.

She has this idea about giving honest feedback and doesn't seem to notice or care that she's insulted half the people in this room. I'm glad I won't be seeing her again.

I know if I reveal something in the team meeting that actually concerns me, he'll cross examine me about it and I'll wish I hadn't said anything.

I don't even notice she's there sometimes. I can't imagine her leading a project.

He always agrees with the boss. Can't he think for himself?

He arrives at the last minute and then expects to take over, as if I'm the warm-up act.

I always cover for her with clients. It was really embarrassing last week when she brought the wrong slides. I'd made sure I brought the right ones for her.

This sort of feedback is not usually given face to face and we are left to infer how colleagues and clients encounter us from their behaviour. When I am confronted with their experiences of me directly, it can come as a shock and be difficult to relate to. Here is an example.

> Philip, an experienced, internal performance management consultant met with a new group of colleagues to work on the delivery of streamlined public services in their locality. He introduces himself as committed to helping them by bringing his practical common sense, track record of making things happen, and a sharp sense of humour.
>
> He sits back and speaks very little during this first meeting. He takes lots of notes and maintains a poker face. This is his usual behaviour when meeting new people. By the end of the meeting he feels he has to say something about how disorganised the meeting has been and points out that they won't meet their targets unless they get their act together. He makes a joke about bringing in someone more experienced to steer the project.
>
> This isn't well received and a senior line manager informs Philip that the only things he's seen Philip bring to this meeting are premature and condescending judgements. Maybe what is needed is a better internal consultant?

Training courses on media and presentation skills offer a way to access direct feedback about how others encounter me, albeit in very specific situations. Typically, such courses coach participants in how to overcome their fear of speaking to an audience or to camera; how to relax and be confident by preparing; how to stay on message and not be tricked or side tracked; and how to make your body language work for you. They urge us to plan and practice for our performances by having a rehearsal, in front of a mirror if necessary. Even then, the unexpected can derail the most orchestrated of presentations, as happened with President George Bush and the shoe-throwing incident. (BBC News, 2008, http://news.bbc.co.uk/1/hi/7782422.stm last accessed 29 January 2013.)

It would be impossible to try and bring this amount of effort and forethought about how I present myself to my everyday working life. It would also be bizarre. Few situations are as controlled and contrived as a presentation. Even a radio or TV interview is a different matter, with the possibility of substantial and unscripted dialogue. How will I react if I don't like a question or feel this is outside what was agreed? The film director Quentin Tarantino was interviewed by a British TV journalist about violence in his film *Django Unchained* and real life violence. (See the report in The *Guardian* newspaper, 11 January 2013.) When asked about the links between enjoying film violence and real violence, Mr Tarantino snarled "Don't ask me a question like that, I'm not biting". He refused the interviewer's attempts to pull him into a debate and told him flatly: "I'm here to sell my movie. This is a commercial for the movie, make no mistake ..."[1]

Some newspapers described Mr Tarantino as losing his cool and as "49 going on 14" (The Independent, 13 January 2013). Another commentator took *the journalist* to task for not challenging Mr Tarantino on the point about selling the movie, perhaps because it was true! Mr Tarantino wasn't being interviewed about a news story, it was about giving him some air time to promote his film. During the interview, viewers could see the journalist looking for his next question by quickly flicking through pages of notes. See link in end note.[2]

This was great adversarial TV. The video clip went viral on social media. It shows us how presence emerges in the moment, an outcome of interactions between me and you, each of us bringing our own (mis)understandings about why we are there and what is expected. This encounter also shows us some of the routines that both the interviewer and Mr Tarantino fall back on when things don't go according to plan (respectively, leafing through reminder notes and refusing to answer questions). Did Mr Tarantino lose his cool? Did the interviewer stick to his questions regardless? Did either of them go home and think:

"I could have handled that better",
"Who does he think he is? It was my interview".
"I lost it there. What happened?"

Both of them have the advantage of being able to watch themselves on video and perhaps glimpse how they were encountered by the other. Those of us who aren't usually filmed in our work have to find other ways to catch sight of our presence and its impact on others.

3.2 What is presence?

Presence is about:

- "being there" (Kahn, 1992), in different situations, at different times, with different people and
- how I choose to bring myself to each of those situations (Berg, 2002).

Some argue that presence is consistent over time and place and that consultants should aspire always to being "fully present". This confuses presence with being present—the extent to which I am paying attention to what I am doing and what's happening (Schneider, 2008, p. 60). My presence when I am negotiating contracts may be different from my presence when I am giving a presentation to clients or planning work with colleagues. My presence at home may be unlike my presence at work, where I exile my cheerful and chatty persona and bring my serious and uncompromising self to the fore. I can be fully present in each of these situations and yet my presence may be very different.

This contextual quality might suggest that presence can be selected, chosen and changed at will. But presence is social. It is forged in psychic space, in the way you and I relate to each other, here and now. Presence is not an attribute of the individual but is a negotiated outcome between those present, a negotiation in which some are more influential than others. How I bring myself to my work may be influenced as much by whom I'm working with and what we are working on as my own preferences about how I am encountered.

Presence is inescapable. Whilst I may not be present (because I am daydreaming, lost in myself, preoccupied or otherwise not engaged in what is going on) I always have presence, whether intended or unintended. The comedian whose jokes fall flat, the consultant who bears no resemblance to the superwoman depicted on her website, and President Obama's poor showing at the first televised debate for his 2012 re-election, are examples of a mismatch between intended and unintended presence. The consultant who bores her client and the CEO who speaks falteringly of his company's bright future don't intend that others encounter them in these ways. But unintended presence isn't always problematic. Sara, the project manager, who surprises herself and others by turning around a difficult meeting, may receive feedback like "I didn't think you had it in you" and "That was great! I'd like to see more of that Sara". Because presence is inescapable, knowing how my colleagues and clients encounter me is a core consulting competence. Finding ways to do that can be a challenge.

On the P3C programme, we designed sessions specifically to offer and receive feedback on each other's presence and we describe some of these in detail in this book. Box 3.2 lists some of the ways my presence is described by participants of The Tavistock Institute P3C programme.

Box 3.2 My presence
In my professional life, my presence has been described in many ways, including:

• containing	• scary
• curious	• authoritative
• challenging	• playful
• helpful	• angry

This feedback helps raise my awareness of my presence (of how others encounter me) and gives me opportunities to develop my presence as an essential tool of my work. But these are not only characteristics of me. They are expressions of how others encounter me and this has significant implications for my consulting practice. I need to think about how my clients and colleagues might experience me and how my presence helps or hinders my crafting a context that is both appropriately reassuring and sufficiently challenging to support their work, development, and change. This requires me to work with my presence as intervention, presence that is designed to help something happen.

To consult effectively, I need to own my presence. I need to think about my presence as the active presentation of myself in relation to my clients and colleagues and the task(s) we are working on, rather than the passive transmission of cues about who I am and what we are doing (Rettie, 2005).

> Davide, a media strategist and internal consultant in a fast paced Italian telecoms company, is much respected technically and works well with his colleagues. Clear thinking and perceptive, he is often asked to join project teams to restructure a department, grow market share, or change technologies. He has been in the same role for several years but is never invited to lead a project.
>
> Davide knows that when faced with uncertainty and surprise his confidence disappears and his self-esteem falls. He thinks of himself as "not good enough". His routine is to mentally search for models and frameworks to tell him what is happening or what to do. The result is that he retreats into his head and isn't present. At critical moments, his colleagues encounter his presence as withdrawn and disinterested or frozen. No-one had said anything to challenge Davide but the implied feedback is "It's OK. That's how you are". Davide feels trapped with a presence that doesn't serve his needs and that he cannot escape from. Maybe it serves the needs of his colleagues, in some way?

Presence emerges in the negotiated space between my needs and anxieties and your needs and anxieties over time. This space may be tightly or loosely regulated, routinised, and ritualised. Our encounter may be unique or ongoing and we may be aware of (and able to speak to) our needs and anxieties or not. It is unlikely that we have ever contracted for or even discussed each other's presence and what would help and hinder our collaboration (Walsh & Whittle, 2009).

> Anwar holds the role of Dean in an international business school. He is thought of as entrepreneurial, having introduced several successful new programmes and raised the profile of the school through his own publications and consulting work. He wants to leave the business school in a better place than he found it and feels the weight of responsibility for its vocational and academic standing.
>
> Well read, he describes himself as "a perfectionist" and expects high standards of others, possibly too high. He knows he is encountered by his colleagues as bossy and critical and obsessively focussed on getting the task done (however he defines it). He wastes little time thinking about his impact on them. Their behaviour (following his instructions, fighting with him, ignoring and hiding from him) puzzles him and confirms his views that it is up to him to lead this group and get the job done.
>
> On a professional development course, participants eventually tell him what his colleagues couldn't, that his presence squeezes them out and rules out any roles for them other than to comply with his orders. Rather than bringing himself in this "take no prisoners" way, can he develop a more collaborative and less competitive presence?

Noticing what is surprising, hurtful or pleasing in the feedback from colleagues and from clients, if they will give it, can help raise awareness of how I encounter myself. The gaps between how I encounter myself, how others encounter me, and how I would like to be encountered comprise a potential space for developing professional presence. But sometimes, even though I want to change how I am encountered, my presence is shaped by how others relate to me.

> Eva is an aerospace specialist in a global consulting firm. With an outstanding track record and years of experience, she works with authority in her areas of expertise but feels trapped in an "expert" role. She has noticed that colleagues don't hang around for a chat once the work is done. They just want her know-how. She wishes she could be allowed to bring other aspects of herself to work, her fun loving and frivolous side, rather than having to be serious all the time.

My presence is designed to feel comfortable: well worn, like a skin or some old clothes. It might not be as pretty or as impressive or as effective as I would like, but it's familiar, reliable, even if I wish it was different. It's unusual to think actively about presence, the way I bring myself to my work, as a core consulting competence. Working with presence as intervention is about understanding the me/not me dynamics, that we spoke about in Chapter One of this book. These dynamics can trip up consultants and change agents and pull us into "presence traps", as illustrated by Philip, Anwar and Eva above.

Presence traps occur when I lose ownership of my presence and my capacity to choose how I bring myself to my work. I risk being stuck with a presence that fails to serve me well in my professional life because it does not adequately affirm my sense of myself. This can happen if my presence has fallen out of my consciousness and I am on autopilot, not noticing how others encounter me. Presence traps can also arise when: I am on the receiving end of powerful projections about my presence (think of school teachers, politicians and TV news readers); I have become lazy and neglectful about sustaining my presence with colleagues and clients (think of rock stars and movie stars); I am having to try very hard to be something I am not (think of whistleblowers, ex-military personnel).

Are you in a presence trap? Work down the list of indicators in the analytic below to see if any sound familiar.

Analytic Presence traps.

	Yes	No
I always end up taking the role of … (devil's advocate, clown, presenter, doom merchant, social secretary) in this group and I'm bored with it/resent it/tired of it.		
My confidence in my competence can be knocked easily.		
People often describe me as … and I don't understand why.		
It's usually me who says the unsayable/the nice things/the apologies.		
I'm so busy doing this job, I haven't got time to think about my presence.		
I don't usually risk saying what I think/what I know/what I feel.		
I have to work very hard to appear to be (… something I'm not …) and I'm exhausted.		
You can't please all the people all the time but it would be good to please … (my boss/my colleague/my client) sometimes.		
People know what to expect from me and, if they don't like it, well that's their problem.		
Usually, I wait to be asked/until last/after the event before I speak or offer suggestions.		
I find I do most of the talking/the decision-making/the planning/the contracting.		
I wish other people would do more rather than wait for me to take the lead.		
I dread working with … (him, her, them, that equipment) in case I make a fool of myself.		
I don't manage my time well. I try to fit in with others instead of speaking up.		
I can't help it, I find it really hard to concentrate in those meetings and I just drift off.		
Can you add any of your own?		

32 RESOURCE-FUL CONSULTING

In any situation, there is no one "best" presence. We have found, when working in consulting and change, that the Principle of Equifinality applies whereby "a system can reach the same final state from different initial conditions and by a variety of different paths" (Katz & Kahn, 1978, p. 30). There are many ways to bring myself to a client situation and be present that can be effective. When you have a moment, take a look at this video clip featuring Itay Talgam talking about great conductors and the differences in their presence http://www.ted.com/talks/itay_talgam_lead_like_the_great_conductors.html?%09 (TED Global, 2009. Last accessed 23 September 2013).

3.3 What shapes presence?

On receiving an invitation to a wedding or other event, many of us will be familiar with the phrase "your presence is requested …". In addition to being there, the invitation may hold other clues about how you might bring yourself to the event: dress codes; timings; the activities to be expected and the location. Such cues help us to make choices about how to present ourselves in ways that will be appropriate and help us take up our roles effectively (Krantz & Maltz, 1997). The mother of the bride does not usually dress like the bridesmaids! But there are few situations as ritualised and where presence is as prescribed as weddings. So what shapes presence in less regulated and more negotiated and ambiguous contexts?

3.3.1 Authority dynamics

Throughout Chapter Two, we worked with identity dynamics as potent shapers of presence. In this chapter, we describe authority dynamics and how they shape professional presence. We have found three, in particular, that can significantly contaminate presence. These are the dynamics of confidence, competition, and control.

Authority emerges in the relationships between roles, tasks, and boundaries. Its particular form and character is governed by:

- How clearly roles are understood, tasks defined and the boundaries of roles and tasks maintained.
- How these can be changed, who can change them and how.
- The resources, rituals, and routines that are available and in place to maintain or change roles, tasks and boundaries (Hirschhorn, 1988).

Authority can be clear, offering containment for difficult tasks and problematic roles. It can also be ambiguous or contested. *The Apprentice* TV show[3] offers many examples where someone who is appointed as project manager for a task is unable to influence team members or control choices. Sometimes, the authority of the project manager is contested by another member of the team who considers him/herself more competent or more experienced or more deserving and competition ensues. At other times, the project manager loses his/her confidence and then their authority. The team finds itself adrift, without the containment of knowing who does what or how.

The ways in which each of us takes up and exercises our authority reflects our own experiences of authority relations when we were young and the ways in which we were managed and controlled by those we experienced as "in authority". In adulthood, it is impossible to predict who will be relatively passive and succumb to the wishes of others and who will take a more authoritarian stance and expect to have their wishes followed (Jacobs, 2005). Passive-aggressive is a combination of the two and has a number of modes. It is indicated by someone taking up the "yes ... but" position in response to a request, direction, or suggestion. Another variant of the passive-aggressive exercise of authority is where someone seems naïve or innocent but has the capacity to evoke strong feelings of anger and frustration in others. This is an example of a projection dynamic, which we discussed in Chapter Two. A third mode of passive aggressive behaviour is signalled by withdrawing or non-participation.

> An articulate and well-educated risk management specialist, James has gravitas. When he speaks, people listen. But he doesn't speak very often. Someone describes him as sulking and as having a brooding presence. Everyone knows that a meeting won't start until he arrives or that a decision will not be made until and unless James indicates his agreement, however indifferently.

On the next few pages, we look further at confidence, competition, and control, three frequently occurring authority dynamics that shape presence and practice.

3.3.2 Confidence

The word confidence comes from the Latin "confidere" to trust in someone or something. I may trust the methods I use, the people I work with, or myself. If I "trust the process" I have confidence that the way my consulting work is designed and delivered is fit for purpose, even though there may be some doubters and cliffhangers along the way. If I take you into my confidence, I trust you. Self-confidence is trusting oneself to do something; to behave appropriately; to contract effectively; to leave with dignity; to intervene with authority.

But self-confidence can become over-confidence, wherein there is no room for doubt and therefore no room for development. If I am overconfident, I do not entertain the possibility of failure. I can be experienced by others as arrogant. Conversely, the absence of confidence implies a lack of trust, in a group, a method, an intervention design, a client, or myself. This can evoke anxieties and ways to defend against the worry of uncertainty, disapproval, and potential failure.

> Karl is always well prepared. A performance improvement specialist, he likes to find out as much as he can about his clients before working with them. He thinks through each meeting before hand, making detailed notes to remind himself not only of what to do but why this is a good idea. His presentation slides always have full notes pages. It is his practice to arrive very early to make sure everything is ready for workshops or training sessions and he makes notes on the way home, just in case he needs to refer to the day's events later.
>
> Karl doesn't trust himself to access his own knowledge and expertise in the moment. His preoccupation with preparation makes him resentful of clients and colleagues who "just turn up and get on with it". His felt authority comes from anticipating and planning. He feels exposed and loses confidence if something unexpected happens. He prefers to consult on his own and tends not to work with anyone else for very long.

Small incidents and experiences can significantly affect my own self-confidence and the confidence I have in others. If I have less time than I thought to make a pitch, if the microphone doesn't work, or if there are building repairs being carried out in the room next door, my belief that I can do a good enough job can be shaken. Sometimes these unexpected events can become useful repositories for doubts that I have already but which I have not acknowledged. Such "unthought knowns" (Diamond, 2008) about my lack of confidence in myself can suffuse my whole presence.

> Lisa is a high profile change project manager in banking. She has become a change manager only recently and finds it difficult to have much confidence in herself. She is surprised when she finds herself taking risks, saying the unsayable to those senior to her and supporting any individual given a hard time by directors. She makes herself available as a friendly face if anyone needs to talk things over or work through a difficult challenge. Her 'unthought known' is that she imagines others do not find her convincing in her new role either. So she tries to be helpful. Perhaps then they might be less inclined to be critical of her?

In Chapter One we described how transitional objects can help to manage these sorts of anxieties and free up the self to be present in ways much more supportive of the tasks in hand. Transitional objects come in many forms. In the examples above, Karl's preparations helped to contain his anxieties. Lisa has constructed a role of rescuer that also serves to rescue herself from the anxieties of her daunting new role. I know a strategy consultant who relies on having access to a bottle of mineral water and drinks slowly from it, occasionally, to calm his fears from time to time. Some consultants take on a different appearance, develop mannerisms or use a "work" voice to maintain their confidence in their professional selves. Do you?

> Lawrence had learned that if he speaks slowly and quietly people stop to hear what he is saying. He uses this technique when he wants to slow down what is happening in workshops and maintain his confidence in his capabilities.

Confidence can develop into the arrogance of overconfidence and a sense of superiority and felt disregard for clients and/or colleagues. Arrogance can be a maladaptive strategy (Crombie, 1993) for protecting a wounded and fragile self; a self that hides behind a grandiose and authoritarian presence.

> A successful OD consultant, Hannah gossips about her clients with her colleagues, her friends and in her professional network. She makes fun of her clients' appearance. She makes comments about whether she does or doesn't like them and whether they are smart and manipulative or thick and to be manipulated. She isn't at all averse to manipulating them, to meet her own needs for respect, for adulation, for superiority.

Analytic Confidence dynamics.

> Take a few moments and remember one or two occasions when confidence was a problem in your work. This might be your self-confidence (too much or too little) or confidence in the way you practice or the techniques you use.
>
> Occasion one
>
> Occasion two
>
> What contributed to the confidence problems?
>
> If confidence remains a problem, how do you think your anxieties shape your authority and your presence?

3.3.3 Competition

Western societies are becoming more competitive. A ranking mentality prevails, in which everyone is designated a winner or a loser. Losers face marginalisation and exclusion, the modern day untouchables.

Competition occurs when there is:

- a contest, conscious, or unconscious, to secure what are believed to be scarce resources, such as an attribute or characteristic, or a position in a social, economic, or psychological ranking;
- a felt need to defend against feelings of inferiority.

> Tina is the director of strategic change in a media organisation. She is quick to understand a situation and used to handing difficult trade union negotiations. She manages her anxieties by writing notes during meetings. This helps her to maintain a careful and considered presence in working situations she describes as battlefields. Tina has noticed she is more and more silent in meetings, working furiously inside herself to come up with the perfect comment or intervention. She wants to be more present by saying what she thinks and feels, rather than sitting in silence until she can think of something that will wow people.
>
> Her company has a reputation for a quick turnover of directors and Tina knows she is only as good as her current performance. She believes she is being evaluated all the time, and this is true for she is constantly judging herself. She is in competition with her ideal self, someone who says things that will stop people in their tracks and make her, and her peers, feel that she is the best.

Some people make a career out of criticising others because they don't feel they are good enough to make it themselves.

> Anton has a reputation for saying what's wrong with a plan, an action, or a person. This is especially the case with people he perceives as powerful. The desire to expose them and confront their half-baked ideas is almost irresistible. He suddenly became very aware of his critical stance and disruptive presence when someone said to him "You always jump on people and close things down. Can't you be more positive sometimes?"

Feelings of inferiority fuel imagined victories over others that take place only in Anton's inner world. These feelings tend to develop in childhood. Experiences of not being as good as someone else, or of being told you are not as good as someone else, are taken up as identity narratives. But sometimes inferiority feelings can be motivational, leading people to succeed in sport, business, and everyday life, against all expectations. The motivation is to avoid the feelings of inferiority, that sense of being less than another. The clearest indicator of inferiority is being ignored or overlooked, as if I don't exist. Not being seen or acknowledged can be more painful than direct rejection. Sometimes, it's easier to disappear before this happens.

> Edward is a coach and organisational change consultant with a small consulting firm in the Netherlands. He knows himself well: which of his own attributes help and hinder his work; the types of personalities that appeal to him and the ones he finds difficult; and what stirs up his anxieties. When he is very anxious, Edward becomes preoccupied with evaluating himself and is no longer present in his work. He is concerned about this self obsession. He wants to find ways to sustain his engagement with others and be more present and available to his clients by switching off his judgemental inner voice.

Consultants manage their anxieties about competition, about being judged, found wanting or rejected, in different ways, some more successfully than others. Gary uses, and perhaps overuses, the term "we" rather than "I" to reduce the felt distance between himself and his big spend, global clients. Melanie works in heavy engineering, in process improvement and whole life costing, and uses humour to contain her anxieties about not being noticed and possible rejection. The feedback she gets is that she is not serious enough. She says "But that is the problem, I am deadly serious". Humour helps to put some distance between Melanie's need to be taken seriously, to be able to compete with others, and her experiences of being taken lightly, of not being a competitor. At the same time, it undermines her authority as a serious player.

Analytic Competition dynamics.

When do you get pulled into competitive dynamics?

Are there some people you just can't help but criticise or situations where you tend to find yourself seeing only problems and short comings? What do you do?

What do your (re)actions do to your authority?

Do people pay more or less attention to you?

What would be a good outcome for you in a competitive situation? What would this mean for your presence?

3.3.4 Control

The dynamics described under confidence and competition could be relabelled dynamics of control. Many things we do involve the exercise of power and influence to achieve control over something, over someone, over myself. Sometimes being in control and the avoidance of being out of control become needs in themselves, needs that shape my authority and presence. Control takes many forms. Control dynamics associated with authority often become visible in groups which are allocated tasks but the methods for working on those tasks are not given, not agreed, or are contested. Here, control can be confused with authority.

> Manuel likes to lead project groups. He wants to make sure they deliver to time and budget and that the job is well done. It will probably mean working extra hours and some sleepless nights to make sure he is on top of things, but that comes with the responsibility. Some of his colleagues don't like responsibility. It is difficult to be friends with people *and* make sure the work is done. Somebody had to do it and he can't imagine anyone else leading the project.
>
> Katarina wishes someone else would take up the project lead role. She has worked with Manuel a few times and had some pretty heated moments. It was like being back at school. He was the project lead but that didn't mean he knew everything nor had authority over everything and everyone. Sometimes a more collaborative approach to working on the tasks and allocating responsibilities would be much more effective, and probably better for Manuel's health.[4]

Taking control without the authority to do so is risky. In this type of situation, consultants may strive to exercise control by taking it from those with formal authority, with consequences for how they are encountered.

> Having just completed another development programme, Johnny is keen to bring his new found understanding of regressive group behaviours into his client work. He'd worked hard to grapple with the theory and understand how to intervene effectively. He now considers himself something of an expert. His boss is very experienced and known for being able to help clients with challenging and potentially destructive group problems. When they next work together, Johnny is surprised and disappointed that he is not given an opportunity to use his new knowledge and lead the session, particularly when it is clearly relevant. In fact, it could help his boss out of a sticky moment. Johnny speaks up, offering his analysis of what is happening and explaining why his boss is not in control. Unfortunately, Johnny's preoccupation with control meant he couldn't see that he was subject to the same regressive group behaviours as everyone else.

When there is anxiety about my capacity to contain my emotions, control can be used to manage the potential threat of revealing my feelings, whether frustration, disdain, loss, love, embarrassment or envy.

> Always aiming to improve his practice, Brian has a formidable repertoire as an OD consultant. He is keen to share his models, theories and designs with the expectation that others will share theirs. This assumption, that other people are like him, pervades his approach to working with colleagues but does not serve him well. He is often disappointed and annoyed that people don't meet his standards. He starts to play things closer to his chest, deliberately not revealing the extent of his know-how and resources to retain control over his feelings.

For some of us, the felt need is not so much to be in control but to avoid responsibility for controlling what happens. We can always find ways to de-authorise ourselves so that no-one takes notice of what I say or do by:

- Asking for permission to say or do something "If it's OK with you …"
- Looking at someone else (usually the person with authority) before I speak or make a decision

- Changing my mind at the slightest resistance
- Making a joke of a serious intervention
- Getting pulled into a pair dynamic with one other person in the room.

Control used to undermine, rather than take up, your authority was described to me by one consultant as "working hard to be in the water rather than on the river bank". Her presence is of someone who talks too much, who thrashes about with making much progress. Sometimes, she keeps her knowledge and competence well hidden. The impact of her presence is that colleagues do not listen to her ideas or want to work with her for very long.

Analytic Control dynamics.

> Identify a few situations when you have felt the need to take control.
>
> Now identify when you have felt the need to avoid being in control of what is happening.
>
> What strategies do you usually use to exercise control?
>
> What strategies do you use to avoid being in control?
>
> Describe how you think others encounter you in these situations.

Now revisit all three authority dynamics that shape presence (confidence, competition, and control) and complete the next analytic, the presence index.

Analytic Presence index.

CONFIDENCE	Y-Yes	N-No
I can rely on my experiences as data		
I wait to be asked to speak/intervene		
I use theory to help to make sense of what is happening		
My confidence in my competence can be knocked easily		
I need my peers to affirm my competence		
COMPETITION		
I maintain my curiosity and welcome surprises		
I can face "not knowing"		
I can use competition rather than be used by it		
I am not derailed by rejections		
I entertain the possibility that I am wrong		
CONTROL		
I always keep the task I am working on in mind		
I use time as a containing device		
I sometimes allow myself to be seduced by powerful others		
Lack of structure makes me anxious		
I have routines to draw on when I need to contain myself		
I use data to inform my actions		

Now discuss your analysis with someone who has a variety of experiences of your professional presence—colleagues, clients, or supervisors.

Take note of:

- what others confirm about your presence that you already know
- any surprises about how authority dynamics shape your presence
- feedback about the impact of these authority dynamics on others.

3.4 Presence intended and unintended

Presence is about "being there" (Kahn, 1992), in different situations, at different times, with different people and how I choose to bring myself to each situation (Berg, 2002). As presence is social, an outcome of interactions between myself and others, it has an element of unpredictability. How people encounter me may or may not be in line with my intentions.

My intended presence may be in tension with:

- presentations of myself I am aware of and want to avoid (which are known from experience, from feedback, or from coaching or development courses)
- presentations of myself I am unaware of (the routines, habits and compulsions I have learned over time and which are subconscious)
- presentations of myself that are imposed or given (such as my age, colour, gender, nationality, accent, job title, reputation).

I have a dog, Hendrix, a big-eyed, lively Springer Spaniel that people are drawn to. He has a lovely presence! I think he's so well behaved he can go anywhere. Overtime we have negotiated, through treats and scolds, how he behaves or presents himself when we go for a walk, drive in the car, or go to the pub. But if the context changes, perhaps another dog pays Hendrix unwanted attention or is playing with a ball that Hendrix wants, we can encounter him as badly behaved. He may not think so and will remain unaware of how he is encountered by us unless we can bring our concerns to his attention. Of course, I can't have a conversation with Hendrix about his presence. Such conversations can be just as challenging with people. The idea of intended and unintended presence can be difficult to comprehend.

> Trevor is infuriatingly helpful. He opens doors, pulls out chairs, notices when lights need switching on or air-conditioning off, and chases up tea and lunch orders. He is so preoccupied with being helpful that he participates little in the discussions and activities of the professional development programme he has joined. It is as if he has taken up an un-contracted, caretaker role that will align him with programme staff and exclude him from the need to participate and learn. But this unintended presentation (of escapee or avoidant participant) is noticed and his self-exclusion becomes the focus of attention; not at all what he intended.

The potency of these unintended presentations varies with context and circumstance. Aged eighteen, I entered a bar with a male friend. Unknown to us, it was an all-male bar. There was a terrific noise and I was booed out! In that situation, my presence preceded me. It was imposed and I was unable to influence how I was encountered. No amount of training or development would have helped. I could only withdraw.

Figure 3.1 shows the relationship dynamics between these elements of presence: intended, unintended, imposed, negotiated, encountered and not encountered.

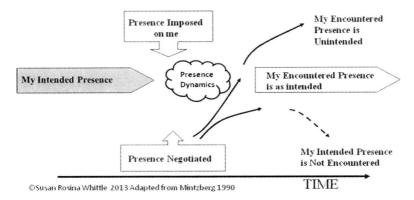

Figure 3.1 Presence intended and unintended.

- An intended presence is that which corresponds to how I want others to encounter me—for Trevor, this was as a staff member, not a learner on a development program. For Trevor to be encountered this way would have required collusion (conscious or unconscious) by actual program staff.
- A negotiated presence arises in the course of interaction, as Trevor's did, at least temporarily. A negotiated presence may be sustained and survive as the encountered presence, or be challenged and confronted as inappropriate.
- An imposed presence is what Susan encountered in the all-male bar. She became the focus of attention and persona non-grata! This was outside her control, something like a forced error in tennis where, no matter how good you are, you are just unable to keep the ball in play.
- An unintended presence is a by-product or parallel of what I intend. In the example above, this was "Trevor the irritating" rather than "Trevor the helpful" as he intended. But unintended presence can also be encountered when we "rise to the occasion" or "push the boundaries" and behave functionally outside our usual repertoires.

Where intended presence is realised, I experience no surprises. I am able to conjure up and control how I am encountered time after time. If I am very attached to this presence, I will find ways to defend it, and there is little chance of development and change. With a less deliberate and more emergent approach, in which presence is negotiated in the moment and unintended presentations of myself encountered, I am in a potentially more creative space. Here I can explore new ways to "be there" and bring my professional self to work.

Whilst these streams of presence have been laid out as discrete options, in reality they mutually configure all the time, as we engage with others in the moment. Presence dynamics are always in tension. If I find the more open and negotiated way I bring myself to our meeting is met by your clinging to how you always bring yourself to our meetings, I may step back into my own routines.

Now complete the next analytic by thinking of experiences and situations in which your presence has been predominantly: (1) as you intended; (2) imposed by others; (3) negotiated in the moment; or (4) surprisingly unintended.

Analytic Streams of presence.

Presence	Experience/situation
1. My presence was as I intended when …	
2. My presence was imposed by others when …	
3. My presence was the result of negotiations when …	
4. My presence was surprisingly unintended when …	

These streams of presence (intended, imposed, negotiated, and unintended) configure how I am encountered every time I bring myself to work. The four are in tension and mould presence simultaneously: sometimes one prevails and at other times a different stream prevails. This figure and ground dynamic is in perpetual motion and can shift in an instant in response to the behaviours, perceptions, and emotions evoked by consulting and change. This shifting configuration can be experienced by both consultant and client and typically emerge when either is faced with:

- Challenges to identity
- Anxieties about being judged and of judging
- Experiences of loss and uncertainty
- Threatening encounters with risks, and manipulation
- Ambiguous roles and relationships
- Others clinging to safe routines and behaviours.

Here's an example of someone taking action to retain ownership of her presence, by choosing how she brings herself to the situation, in the face of it being imposed through association with others.[5]

> The only time I put on lipstick is to avoid walking in with people I work with.

All too often, consultants are ill prepared to work with the emotional entanglements of presence dynamics (Benjamin, 1998). This can undermine both the consultant's and the client's capacity to be present and hinder the practice of consulting and change. Figure 3.2 shows some of the entanglements that can shape how I am encountered by others.

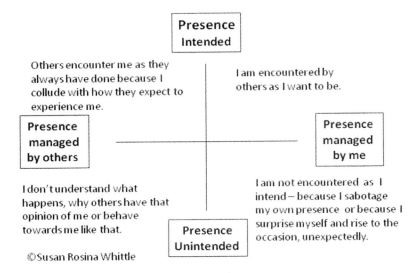

Figure 3.2 Encounters and entanglements.

Individuals and groups engage in behaviours that are unintended and sometimes unconscious, arising from the unspoken and often unacknowledged anxieties of those present. All too easily, I can find my presence shaped by another's intent, rather than my own, and I become a part in someone else's script. My presence can be caught by the dynamics of the encounter pulling on my identity, for example when I take up the role of the knowing leader, the fool, or cynic. I can even be pulled into competition for one for these roles. Or I may take flight from a difficult task or awkward moment by withdrawing or pulling rank, either to save face or take the blame.

Being aware of how emotional entanglements shape my presence is an essential consulting competence but where do they come from? In Chapter Two we worked on entanglements linked to identity and explored projection and transference. Here we revisit the idea of transference but in relation to presence.

3.5 Presence and transference

In Chapter Two, transference was described as an unconscious process whereby I might relate to another person as if they are someone else, from another time and place.

> *Transference* is the phenomenon whereby we unconsciously transfer feelings and attitudes from a person or situation in the past on to a person or situation in the present. (Hughes & Kerr, 2000, p. 58)

Family figures, figures of love and affection, of hate and rejection, figures of wish-fulfilment and figures that are lost are often evoked in situations which stir up memories and feelings. Some of the comments in Box 3.1 suggest transference at work. Those of us occupying roles as authority figures will be used to attracting feelings from clients, staff, and students, that originate elsewhere. Unintentionally, we find ourselves behaving as a father figure, boss, or teacher from time to time. I might find myself relating to a mature and able management consultant as my son because of an imposed or unintended aspect of his presence; maybe his smile, his height, or his sense of humour remind me of my son.

Have you heard children repeating the words of their mothers and fathers as if their own? Transference means that when others encounter me they may have access not only to my own self but also to those significant others (my mother, father, siblings, teachers, bosses, etc.) that I carry with me and that constitute aspects of myself. These are revealed in my unintended presence. Others also bring important figures from their past into our encounter as their identities are evoked and revealed. This complex field of selves, identities, transference, and countertransference creates a potential space in which presence is shaped and reshaped by what the transference evokes.

We can think about this space as a matrix (See Figure 3. 3) comprised of time and place in which:

- time can be now (the present) or then (the past)
- place can be here (where I am at the moment) or there (another place from the past).

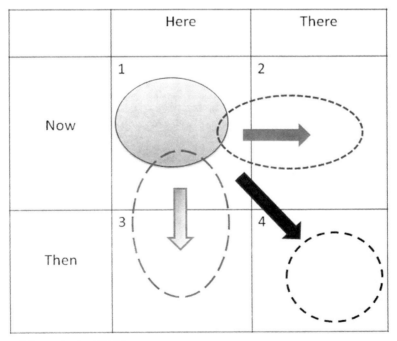

©Susan Rosina Whittle

Figure 3.3 Presence and transference.

Any figures or places from my past or your past may be evoked in the transference between us. For simplicity, the following describes the potential transference relationship between you and me.

- If I am relating to you here (in this place) and now (at this time), I am in quadrant 1 and what might be called fully present (Kahn, 1992);
- If I am relating to you now (at this time) and there (as if we are in another place) I am in quadrant 2 and perhaps thinking about our work with another client or colleague rather than the work in hand. I am transferring my feelings from that into what we are doing at the moment.
- In quadrant 3, I am relating to you here (in this place) and then (at some time when we worked together in the past). Maybe we had a disagreement in this office yesterday which is still unresolved and leaking into today's work.
- In quadrant 4, I relate to you as if then (another time) and there (another place), maybe when I was your boss rather than your client.

If we then add the possibility of my encountering you "as if" you are my father, brother, daughter, ex-boss, old girlfriend, or any other significant figure from my past, and we have the possibility of you encountering me in the same "as if" way, the stage is set for possible confusion and misunderstanding. This is where many problems with presence arise. If I am relating to you as if you are my mother and you are relating to me as if I am your teacher, or friend, we will probably struggle to disentangle how we encounter each other and how we can work well together. Similarly, if I am present in quadrant 3 of Figure 3.3 and you are in 1, my behaviour may seem inexplicable to you.

We all have different propensities for others to stir up thoughts, feelings, and figures from our past. Some things are so deeply buried they are unlikely to be revived. But beware, transference happens at the most unexpected times and places. You know it is transference dynamic when:

- You can say "I have no idea where that came from" about someone's behaviour towards you.
- You find you are withholding yourself from someone or are drawn toward someone inexplicably.
- When you have strong emotions that seem disproportionate to the matter in hand.

Here are some actions to help you own your presence and stay in the here and now:
   Notice:

- What I am feeling
- Who I pay attention to and who I ignore
- What I choose to speak about and what I leave out
- What I respond to and what I dismiss/avoid/ignore
- What my body is doing—hands, head, eyes, voice, feet, legs, posture—and whether I am firmly grounded in the here and now or:

    ○ I have one foot in another time and place
    ○ I am speaking with a voice from my past
    ○ I don't see you but someone else.

Being aware of the potential power of transference to shape presence is essential for mind-ful practice. To own my presence, rather than succumbing to transference dynamics, I need to be in touch with aspects of myself that I may not have revealed but that may be evoked in the moment. This awareness comes with experience and in the working through, with colleagues and shadow consultants, of the "what happened there" moments in consulting work.

3.6 What do I know about my presence?

For Jung, the self has a dual presence: that which is known (the persona) and that which is unknown (the shadow). It is important to recognise the influence of the shadow on practice. In Chapter One, we looked at the Johari window and did some analysis of the four windows in relation to presence, including the blind spot and the unknown quadrants. In this chapter we have examined how presence can be intended and unintended and how emotional entanglements can lead to my presence being managed by others, rather than me.

The shadow self is hidden from others and from oneself. It is disowned, perhaps because it is embarrassing or shameful. It is "not me". For example, whilst immediate feedback might help me to gauge whether people find my jokes funny, I may be unaware of my unintended presence: perhaps I am not taken seriously as my inept attempts at humour are undermining my authority. Disowned aspects of myself (perhaps I gossip about people behind their backs or envy others' success), can influence how others encounter me in ways I may not be aware of or even deny. If others do not reveal how they encounter me, if they collude in hiding or denying how I am encountered, I may continue to be blissfully unaware of my unintended presence. It can remain hidden from me indefinitely and lead to perpetual puzzlement about why I get this or that reaction from people. For those of us consulting to and leading change, this can significantly diminish professional impact and lead to the construction of all sorts of rationales to explain away presence issues. Mary Tolbert describes presence as the use of self with intent (Tolbert, 2006) The more I know about my presence, the more effectively I can use it as an instrument of change in my practice. To use presence as intervention, and myself as an instrument of change, requires some awareness and understanding of:

- how you encounter me and how I encounter myself
- the dynamics that shape that encounter
- which of those dynamics I can work with and which I need to contain.

We have worked with these throughout this chapter. Now try completing the next analytic, listing both desirable and undesirable aspects of your presence. If you can't complete it on your own, have conversations with colleagues and/or with clients.

Analytic What I know about my presence.

When working with my clients, I think desirable aspects of my presence are ...	When working with my colleagues, I think desirable aspects of my presence are ...	My clients describe desirable aspects of my presence as ...	My colleagues describe desirable aspects my presence as ...
When working with my clients, I think undesirable aspects of my presence are ...	When working with my colleagues, I think undesirable aspects of my presence are ...	My clients describe undesirable aspects of my presence as ...	My colleagues describe undesirable aspects my presence as ...

Now collate the results you consider important under the four headings in the chart below:

Any aspects of my presence described as desirable by me, my colleagues and/or my clients	Any aspects of my presence described as undesirable by me, my colleagues and my clients	Any aspects of my presence described as desirable by my colleagues and my clients but not by me	Any aspects of my presence described as undesirable by my colleagues and my clients but not by me

From this analysis, list those aspects of your presence you feel you need to work on. This is your Presence Development Agenda (PDA) Part one.

You might want to think about whether there are aspects of your presence that you feel are lacking, ways to behave and ways to present yourself that would like but are somehow missing or unachievable.

Write them down. This is your Presence Development Agenda (PDA) Part two.

We will be returning to your PDA's in Chapter Seven.

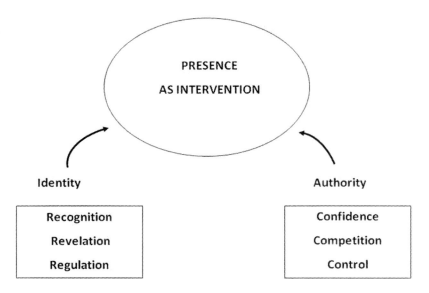

Figure 3.4 Presence as intervention.

3.7 Summary

In Chapters Two and Three we have explored how identity and authority dynamics shape presence. In the practice of consulting and change, presence is an intervention that can help or hinder our work with clients and colleagues, as shown in Figure 3.4.

We have seen how preoccupations can undermine my capacity to use myself as instrument and how practitioners can be caught out by the power of transference and the complications of unintended presence.

For presence to support my practice and client development, I must own my presence since "… the ultimate success of an intervention rests with the practitioner and what one brings to the process. In other words, self is the most important tool of the practitioner". (Tolbert & Hannofin, 2006, p. 70).

Much of our practice takes place in role. In Chapter Four, we turn to role space, both as a resource and a mediator between individual, group, and organisation dynamics in consulting practice.

Notes

1. Watch the interview at http://www.guardian.co.uk/film/2013/jan/11/tarantino-krishnan-guru-murthy?INTCMP=SRCH last accessed 29 January 2013. A full transcript of the interview is also available at http://www.channel4.com/news/tarantino-uncut-when-quentin-met-krishnan-transcript last accessed 21 November 2013.
2. http://www.irishexaminer.com/opinion/columnists/terry-prone/opinion-questions-to-be-asked-about-celebs-right-not-to-reply-219456.html 01/14/2013 last accessed 28 January 2013.

3. http://www.bbc.co.uk/programmes/b007qgcl/clips
4. If you recognise this scenario, have a look at Roberts, V. Z. (1994). The Self-assigned Impossible Task. In: A. Obholzer & Roberts Vega Zagiessr (Eds.), *The Unconscious at Work* (pp. 110–120). London: Routledge.
5. http://www.postsecret.com/ last accessed 2 February 2013.

CHAPTER FOUR

Role space

Karen Izod

Many of the practice dilemmas that we are recounting arise from a sense of being trapped in identities that feel constraining, and grappling with a level of authority that doesn't fit well with the presence that we are trying to bring. As we listen to these stories of practice, then we are in touch with a need for working on an improved sense of space, in ourselves and for our clients, in order to distinguish between:

- Roles that I am given and roles that I am taking
- Now and then, here and there
- Those things that are me and those that I designate as not me.

Working to enlarge and enrich the spaces in which I can operate draws upon my capacities to make sense of my thoughts and feelings, and to regulate them in relation to the behaviours and actions I then attempt. This work which goes on in our inner worlds is a forerunner to working on role.

Role space concerns itself with professional and organisational role, both as an asset to our practice and as a mediator between individual, group, and organisation functioning. Roles can act as the movers of our identities, and the shapers of our presence, and at the same time can impose expectations—the shoulds and oughts of what we do and how we do it. We work with the idea of roles "in the wings" of our practice, there to be taken up and crafted in bringing ourselves to work with the resources afforded by identity and presence.

In Figure 1 in the introduction we locate role space, along with potential space, as providing opportunities for experimentation at the margins of identity, presence, practice and change.

Terms like writer in residence, consultant at large, Minister without portfolio are all examples of where organisations are attempting a less defined, more fluid set of roles, offering the possibility for the professional to engage where and how their attention is taken, and to bring

54   RESOURCE-FUL CONSULTING

their skills to bear at these touch-points. Of course it isn't that long before this space starts to erode, and expectations on both sides, professional and organisational, start to close in, even in these most loosely crafted positions.

Attempting to keep these spaces open, in my own mind, and in the minds of the organisational players I come into contact with, is a mind-ful skill of consulting to change. We can think of role space as providing:

- Space for purposeful, deliberative activity about the nature of the roles that I craft for myself and negotiate with others, that give me some "elbow-room" in how I use my identities and work with my presence
- The qualities of a potential space; room for play and experimentation
- A temporary space to stabilise aspects of role in a period of transition.

This section offers:

- Some perspectives on role, what roles are, how we construct them
- Suggestions for how you can examine role space in your consulting and change activities.

4.1 Thinking my way into role

Taking on a consulting assignment or a change programme requires both an imaginative and empathic approach to what an organisation or a business market is looking for or is in need of. Based on information that I gather about what the assignment entails, and what is required of me, I need to think my way into what might be at stake for the client, what I might find myself doing, and then imagine myself in a place where I am doing it. This is the skill of contracting (see Chapter Five) and will help me decide on whether there is likely to be a good fit between what the work entails, and who and what I am equipped to bring through my identity and

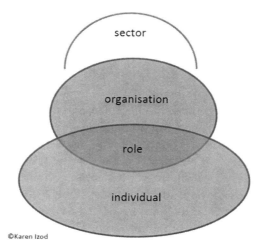

Figure 4.1 Role configuration.

ROLE SPACE 55

presence. This overlap between who I am, and what I bring and the "enterprise" or the work of the organisation is a space for role and role affords us the opportunity to use our identities and our presence as intervention. It is often configured in the overlap between myself as an individual, the organisation I am working in, or relating to, and how that organisation sits in a sector, market, or environment. See Figure 4.1 above.

We can think of role as a construction, in the mind, between:

- What I imagine I am here to do (and how to do it)
- What organisational players (and external stakeholders) also imagine that I am here to do (and how to do it).

It functions as a mediating factor between individual and organisation that shapes the way we think and behave, offering the potential to embrace, or distance myself from these expectations (Simpson & Carroll, 2008).

Figure 4.2 below attempts to show what role looks like in reality, as we bring our constructions of identity, authority, and presence to roles, in relation to tasks, embracing some, distancing ourselves from others. At varying times we will foreground some aspects of our identity, and others will fall to the back. Some tasks will enable us to act with more authority than

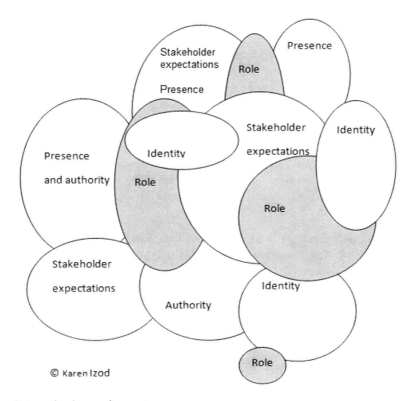

Figure 4.2 Realities of role configuration.

others and to intervene with presence; some stakeholders will be more prominent, depending on where we are in the consulting and change cycle (see Chapter Five).

Here are some aspects of how Reed and Bazalgette (2006) define role:

A role is defined:

- As a person identifies the aim of the system they belong to (role finding)
- Takes ownership of that aim as a member of the system (role making) and
- Chooses the action and personal behaviour which, from their position, best contributes to achieving this aim (role taking).

And here are some pointers as to how Simpson and Carroll (2008) make links between identity and role:

- Identities emerge from the interactions across the boundaries of different knowledge (professional) domains—role is an intermediary device—constructed for the negotiation of identity and difference
- (Role) relates to the construction of identity in a way that also recognises the playful and exploratory potential of multiple unfolding roles.

Working on role issues with our clients suggests that roles are:

Multiple and provisional: As with our identities, we also inhabit multiple roles. How we might behave as a consultant in one setting might be quite different in another, and we may behave differently at different times in the same setting. So roles are provisional, they respond to the culture and needs of the parts of the organisation that we comes into contact with at any one time when attempting to work on a task.

Political: The space that an organisation makes for me to come into may be overly defined, so that there is very little room for personalising how I go about things. Or the role may be too close to another, overlapping so that I am constantly treading on the toes of this person or that. Similarly a role can be so under-bounded and ill-defined that energies are dissipated and work becomes ineffectual.

Contested: Not everyone agrees what a role should look like, or the role itself may hold inconsistencies of expectation. Take bankers and politicians. We may believe that people in these public roles should be trustworthy, keep their private lives private, manage any temptations for personal gain and so on. But we may also expect them to be greedy, lead salacious private lives, and be less than transparent. Which of these sets of expectations does the banker or politician take up? What do they start to identify with as a guiding principle in public life?

4.2 Getting space between role given and role taken

Krantz & Maltz (1997) work with the ideas of role given and role taken, in relation to the way we go about a task, and the feelings that are evoked as we try to work on that task.[1]

People we might never meet, but whose views about how things might or should be done permeate the fields in which I work through documents, stories, hierarchies, and cultures. Expectations filter through layers of communication, our imaginative perceptions and through the roles that we take up to make things happen.

> Moira describes her first position in a consultancy practice: I'm expected to focus on getting new business, and to create lists of organisations to call up and give them a sales pitch. I'm repeatedly told stories of former consultants who made dozens (if not hundreds) of calls for the one that turns into business. I know this isn't the way I want to do it: I want to go to networking events, meet people, start conversations, but this isn't seen as "doing the hard graft". I'm having to prove myself.

Moira is caught here between complying with her organisation's expectations about how she should go about a task, and wanting to bring something that feels more authentic and that she has greater faith in. She faces a challenge in how she might create more space within her role to function with "equivalent reality" (Harris, 2010, p. 22; Izod, 2013, p. 151), to bring herself to this task with an equivalence to what is required, but that is not necessarily the same. She is working here with her own imagination about what the role requires, and the imagination of others in her organisation, and has a choice about the extent to which she embraces the culture of "cold-calling" as a part of her role, or tries to bring her own methods to the fore.

Analytic Expectations between task and role.

Try analysing a consultancy assignment or a change project in relation to the range of tasks that you are undertaking, and the expectations that go with them as to how they might be done.

Task	My expectations	Expectations of others

What does this indicate to you about the complexity of the expectations you are facing as you attempt to work on these tasks?

How congruent, divergent are these expectations?

Where might you need to focus your attention so as to bring yourself (your identity and presence) to these tasks and craft a role that feels sufficiently authentic?

4.3 Getting space between now and then, here and there

It's important to mention here that the kind of space that we are thinking of between now and then, here and there (see Figure 3.3. in Chapter Three), is primarily a space for manoeuvre in our thinking and in our actions. Being in the present, doesn't mean shutting off the past, but working with it as a resource, in the same way that an imagined future can act as a resource that motivates and guides. It is when these dimensions become solidified, and immovable, or when they come to the fore and are transferred between time and place without thinking, that the difficulties of being present, outlined in Chapter Three, start to present themselves.

> As a social worker practicing in the 1970s Mary behaved and thought about herself differently to how she behaves and thinks about herself now in her role as an organisational consultant. She feels able to reveal more about personal interests and family life in her work with her clients now than she did then, in her social worker role. But some things persist over time: the challenge of understanding what might be the social/political dynamics affecting a family as a social worker, also finds a place in the way that she tries to make sense of an organisation.

This is an example of how role can evoke aspects of identity that serve as "props" (Simpson & Carroll, 2008) to the roles that I inhabit. In Mary's situation, she is able to bring some (but not all) of the way she thought about and analysed situations as a social worker to her present role. While she faces new situations as a consultant, and has to bring in new ways of thinking and analysing, she is able to formulate an identity for this work that does not have to start from scratch every time. Aspects of her former identity, on the wings of her present role as a consultant can offer a starting point for her as well as provide containment when facing the unknown.

But role is not a free for all. Role guides and shapes the cluster of identities that we have at our disposal. It requires discipline in the choice of what we can bring and what we need to leave out. If Mary were to start to behave as if she had a statutory authority to intervene with her organisational client, then she would soon be in difficulty. Part of the task of constructing a role is to revisit identity—"who am I", in this situation, and what kind of authority do I bring to be able to work with presence.

When Dorothy says "We're a long way from Kansas, Toto" in *The Wizard of Oz*, (1939) she knows that what she sees and experiences can't be located in the familiar, there is too much of a gap between what is happening in front of her eyes, and what she is able to make sense of. This feeling of being a long way from home is a common one when we are not entirely sure how we have got from A to B, and what it is we are doing. It is tempting to turn strange experience into understandable experience by reducing its complexity, particularly by focussing on what we know how to do, even though it may not be relevant in this moment. Here, thinking about role space, we are concerned with keeping a space open for the deliberative crafting of roles that offer some "elbow-room", but that also can afford some stabilising of roles in a period of flux. This is an example of how role can function at the edges of identity, offering shape to an experience, without overwhelming it, and closing down new opportunities.

> In his new job as CEO of a small charity, Jonathan is invited to speak at a national conference on the vision that his organisation has for the next five years. Being visible, and operating at national level is unfamiliar territory, and Jonathan is worried that although his development policy is sound, he will be unable to present himself with sufficient gravitas to be taken seriously. At the edges of his memory is an experience from early in his career of being a political activist in his local community. He can see that he can retrieve aspects of this role, his conviction, his clear thinking (from its time and place) so as to craft an identity for himself now where he can allow himself more authority to speak.

Analytic Time lines (time to play).

> Draw a picture or a time line to identify times/periods in your life when you have been most open to learning and change.
>
> What was happening at this time, what made these moments significant?
>
> What aspects of these experiences can you retrieve now to bring as assets for your present roles?
>
> This is an activity which lends itself well to working in a group, telling stories about these experiences generally helps to make the link between past and present, and to notice connections that can be helpful.

4.4 Getting space between me and not me

As roles can become the props for identities, so identities can become the props for roles.

A role generally has to wear well, that is, we need enough of a valency—a predisposition or requirement for a role to take it up over any period of time. We are unlikely to take up a role, to choose the actions and personal behaviours which fit best, if they are alien to us. For example, I need to value and be predisposed to detail, for me to take up the part of a role that requires detailed attention. When I find myself taking up a role or a stance that is "not me" or an extreme version of me, then it is time to think about what I might be "taking on" for the organisation. That is, an element of its functioning that for some reason can't be noticed or talked about, and therefore has to be enacted.

Here is an example from Gillian's practice. Gillian is a self-employed consultant working in higher education.

> Gillian is asked to consult to a department in the public sector, which needs to find a sustainable way of working to meet growing expectations for its services. She begins well, meeting with groups of people and gathering a sense of what is proving unsustainable: the need to be entrepreneurial and generate a proportion of their income, and the need to do more with diminishing resources. As time goes on, Gillian finds herself becoming superefficient, fitting more and more into the time that she had contracted to work. She over-expects of herself, and the task starts to feel impossible as she reduces any time for reflection. It would certainly not be sustainable for her to continue effectively in this way.

When Gillian can step away and think about this, and analyses the "what is me/not me" behaviours that she is enacting, then she sees that her own tendency (or valency) to be economical leads her into taking on a role in this consultation of overworking and doing too much. Very clearly, she has had an experience of what it is like to work in this department and she starts to act it out (see Chapter One) in the way that she takes up her consulting role. Working out with her clients what constitutes a manageable workload, and comparing it with others, is a feature of what can't be talked about, and a clue as to what she might need to focus on with them.

If Gillian were applying for a job in this team, it might be described like this: "endlessly energetic team player, willing to work exceptionally long hours, for an indefinite period" but this is not how jobs are advertised. This is what has to be experienced and experimented with, so as not to get stuck in the mix of expectations of herself and others.

These are some of the aspects of the consulting/change agent role that we may have a sense of when we are contracting, but we won't know until we experience them how they will play out over time.

Here are some other "situations vacant" that we find ourselves in:

- "person required to jostle everyone along to make sure the proposal gets in on time"
- "person required to divert trouble away from the boss"
- "person required to take the side of the financial team against operations".

Figure 4.3 Applying for role.

Analytic Working out the me/not me.

> Think about a consulting scenario that you are currently engaged in, and examine your own "modus operandi": how are you going about doing your work?
>
> Think of some words to describe yourself: energetic, procrastinating, having fun, overly detailed, slow, constantly daydreaming, bored.
>
> Turn these into a "situations vacant" to describe the position that you find yourself in. How much of this is me, (what I bring), and how much is evoked by others, and the task in hand?
>
> Where might you want to give yourself more space between me/not me? What might that involve you thinking about or doing?

In Chapter Five, we look at how we bring preoccupations with our identity and presence into our consulting roles, and how our practice is influenced by the emergence of these preoccupations at different stages of the consulting cycle.

Note

1. See http://www.worklab.com/wp-content/uploads/2009/12/Role-Consultation-Article2.pdf

CHAPTER FIVE

Practice

Susan Rosina Whittle and Karen Izod

In this chapter, we look at the preoccupations in practice of some of the consultants we have worked with. This is designed to help you to think about your own preoccupations by identifying:

I. What you do usually, those learned routines and safe, tried, and tested practices.
II. What you don't do usually, because you dare not or cannot and want to.

We use a well known model, the consulting cycle, to explore dilemmas involving identity, authorisation, and presence that tend to occur at different stages of consulting work. These are illustrated by practice vignettes and discussed in relation to some of the thinking and theories we have developed over our professional careers and put to work on the Tavistock Institute Practitioner in Consulting and Change Programme. First, let's remind ourselves of why we are preoccupied with preoccupations!

5.1 Preoccupations

Do I use my identity and presence as resources in my work? Am I mind-ful of or mindless about my presence and identity? For those of us working with change, identity and presence need to be assets. They shape the way I consult by bounding my practice, that potential space in which consultant and client meet to work creatively on tasks, address problems, and realise development. As such, identity and presence comprise foundation resources for consultants tasked with developing clients and changing their organisations.

Practice is also shaped by preoccupations. Preoccupations are what I habitually notice and focus on or what I ignore or avoid. Preoccupations are liabilities, potentially draining and diverting consulting resources into anxiety work.

64 RESOURCE-FUL CONSULTING

> Although it meant she would now have to work the weekend, Alison couldn't resist her "FOMO" and managed to get an invite to a launch event she'd just heard about.
> Are you aware of FOMO or "fear of missing out"?
> It is reported that Harvard Business School students spend thousands of dollars a year going to parties, playing golf, and networking for fear of missing out. The syndrome is described as "a chronic inability to turn down invitations to any party, dinner, or junket attended by anyone who might be a valuable addition to one's network—no matter the cost …. It begins with a pang of envy. Next comes the anxiety, the self-doubt, the gnawing sense of inadequacy … unchecked, it can distract us from our own lives … We forget how to be in the moment … We're too busy tweeting about the scent of those roses actually to breathe it in …" (Anderson, 2011).
> To wrestle control back from your FOMO we are advised to "… take a moment to find the off switch on that smart phone and remind it who's boss, rather than letting it enslave you by exploiting your deeply human anxieties." (Anderson, 2011).

This chapter is designed to help you reach the preoccupation off-switch. Preoccupations trip you up and trap you in compulsive and defensive routines. As such, they offer signposts to developmental needs that you may want to work on, whereby identity and presence become resources rather than liabilities.

Identity preoccupations: We described identity as the characteristics and attributes that offer some coherence to life (whether desirable or not) and which blend into something that is recognisable, to me and to others, as me. To sustain that recognition means making choices about which identities to reveal, to whom, and engaging in identity work, to regulate the emotions that are evoked in sustaining my sense of myself. We find preoccupations with recognition, revelation, and regulation often arise in consulting practice. We explored them in some detail in Chapter Two.

Presence preoccupations: Presence is about being there, in different situations at different times, and about how I choose to bring myself to each of those situations. Presence is inescapable. How colleagues and clients encounter me may not be as I intend, but they do encounter me somehow. How others encounter my presence is shaped by authority dynamics and preoccupations with confidence, competition, and control. We explored these in some detail in Chapter Three.

Preoccupations can easily trip us up or trap us in ineffective practices. Preoccupations can be pursued until some are excessively present and others mindfully absent from our practice and excluded from our repertoires. Preoccupied consulting is impoverished consulting. To enrich your repertoire and practice more mindfully, it is helpful to know when preoccupations are likely to arise and what triggers these defensive routines. The consulting cycle is a useful model for raising awareness about when some typical preoccupations might be encountered.

5.2 The consulting cycle and typical practice dynamics

The stages of the consulting cycle are usually represented in linear sequence, as shown in Figure 5.1.

In reality, the cycle is more emergent, chaotic, and repetitive, as illustrated in Figure 5.2. Stages arise iteratively and consultants usually need to engage with several cycles and several stages simultaneously in their work with any one client system.

We use the term intervention rather than planning and implementation to reflect our view that there is no distinct "doing" stage. *Everything* is an intervention. Sticking to a planned sequence can be unhelpful, putting the brakes on changes which have unanticipated momentum, or moving too quickly without attending to unforeseen delays and regressions. Working with timing and pace are critical to effective consulting (Whittle, 2013). You may have noticed that "learning" and "regression" appear as stages to be worked with. We introduce these more fully in Figure 5.4.

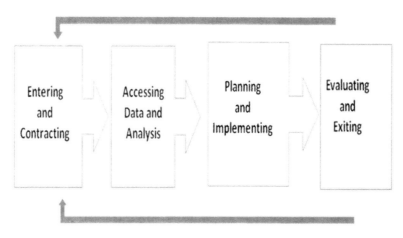

Figure 5.1 Consulting cycle, a linear sequence of stages.
(Adapted from Kolb & Frohman, 1970; Cummings & Worley, 2008).

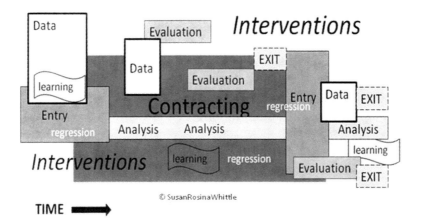

Figure 5.2 Stages of the consulting cycle—the reality.

Frequently, we see consultants preoccupied with some stages of the consulting cycle and avoidant or neglectful of others. A protracted entry and a nominal contracting stage may be followed by prolonged gathering and analysis of data. Some consulting firms (and client organisations) regard the production of a plan as the final stage in a consulting project, with little if any attention paid to interventions, to evaluation, or exit. Examples of consulting cycle profiles, with resources such as people, time, and/or money allocated to stages, are shown in Figure 5.3.

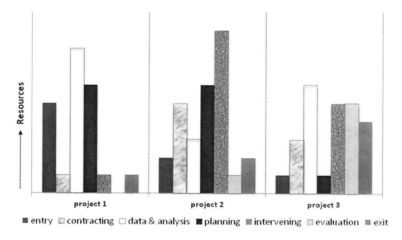

Figure 5.3 Stages of the consulting cycle: preoccupations and neglect.

Analytic Consulting cycle preoccupations.

Are any of the profiles in Figure 5.3 familiar to you?

How would you visualise your own project stages?

Is there a typical or default pattern to your consulting work and if so, which if any stages are missing or avoided?

How does this impact your practice and your potential practice?

We designed the P3C programme around developments of the consulting cycle, structured into five module themes. Linked to each theme are the consulting dynamics we find are strongly associated with each stage of the cycle. These are:

- entry and contracting and the dynamics of power and containment
- data and analysis and the dynamics of credibility and competition
- interventions and the dynamics of risk and accountability
- learning and regression and the dynamics of sustainability
- evaluation and exit and the dynamics of endings and loss.

Preoccupations interact with these consulting cycle dynamics. On the following pages we offer examples of practice problems arising from the interplay of identity and presence preoccupations with consulting cycle dynamics. It's useful to keep in mind that stages are not linear. For example, dynamics of endings and loss don't make themselves felt only during the final exit, nor dynamics of power solely during the initial entry and contracting stages of consulting work. All the consulting cycle dynamics can arise at any time in a consulting contract, as "stages" iterate and are revisited, as shown in Figure 5.2. Knowing in the midst of consulting work that you are once again entering and contracting (perhaps because of the need to change the contract or working with a new department or group), working with new data and analysis, or evaluating work that has already been done, helps us to tune into potential preoccupation problems triggered by the associated dynamics. Let's have a look at each stage.

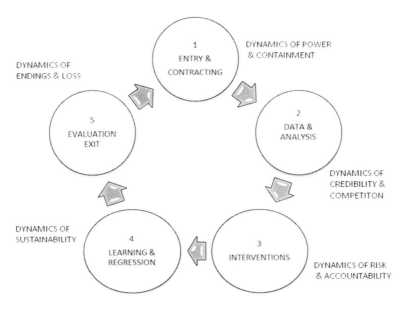

Figure 5.4 P3C module themes and practice dynamics as stages of the consulting cycle.

5.3 Entry and contracting and the dynamics of power and containment

Schein (1990) encourages us to focus on surprises at entry, as surprises offer data about:

- our own assumptions and expectations
- what makes us feel comfortable and what evokes discomfort.

Not having access to those things that help me feel comfortable (the "right" room, appropriate technologies, enough time, a cup of tea), I can become anxious and preoccupied in my discomfort. I might start blaming someone (my colleague or staff, the hotel, the client) for not meeting my expectations or not checking out assumptions.

When contracting, I might feel irritated or uncomfortable:

- when the client or my colleagues are being too pernickety or too laissez-faire about terms
- if I am asked repeatedly to provide the same information or reassurances
- if it's difficult to agree a start date or the focus of the work
- about not being able to find the appropriate person to contract with
- when I am kept waiting—for a meeting, a phone call, a decision.

During entry and contracting, both consultants and clients are coping with this mixture of emotions and their concerns about what will be exposed and what they are able to control.

> Janet is an executive coach in a respected European OD consultancy. She was invited by the HR director of Better Insurance to submit a proposal for an executive leadership coaching program to support rapid market growth. During discussions with the MD, Janet was asked whether she could help with a specific "situation" in which many managers found one senior executive (Stephen) impossible to work with. Could she coach this person right away? Fees and terms were agreed quickly and Janet worked with Stephen to address his difficulties. Three months later, Stephen was fired. Coaching for other executives was never pursued by Better Insurance and Janet was puzzled.
>
> Looking back, she realises Stephen had been made a scapegoat for other problems. Coaching had been a waste of time. Why had she not questioned the MD's description of Stephen as a problem? Janet remembered she had been pleased, if a little anxious, to be contracting with the MD and, rather than making her own analysis, she had accepted her client's version of events. Janet has now lost her authority as an independent consultant and, from entry with the MD, has behaved as an employee.
>
> In conversation with a colleague, she understands that the discomfort she often feels in challenging people she perceives as powerful is rooted in early life experiences. This helps to explain why she has been unable to contain her anxiety about confronting the MD's account and assert her authority.

It is probably during entry and contracting that presence is tested and identity challenged the most. Both consultant and client preoccupations risk being exposed until and unless routines to manage uncertainty and anxiety are re-established. Typical preoccupations are shown in Table 5.1.

Table 5.1 Mixed emotions at entry and contracting.

Consultant preoccupations	Client preoccupations
Confidence: I can't make a difference. I don't have the skills or competence. There is no reward for the effort. It's not me.	**Helplessness**: I have no power to change the situation. I am inadequate. I am a victim.
Distance from the client: We will remain strangers. We will never get close. I'll have to stay totally "in role". Do I belong here?	**Alienation**: No-one in this organisation cares about me nor do I care about them. I don't belong here.
Over identification: I understand entirely and the answer is ...	**Hubris**: I am the one who can fix this ...
Control: They won't or can't tell me what is really happening. I have to depend on them. I am not in control.	**Control**: I have too much information. I can't sort it out or see clearly. I am not in control.

©SRWhittle: Adapted from Block 2000; Cummings and Worley 2008.

These preoccupations can catch out even the most experienced consultant.

> Now in a senior internal consulting role, Patrick still feels a novice. He left a successful career with a global management consulting firm and seems to have lost his authority. He knows he does a good job but is surprised to find how rarely he is called on to contribute any strategic thinking. He has become a change technician rather than a change consultant. Will he ever feel he belongs here and have the confidence to risk challenging his internal client, as he used to as an external consultant?

One difficulty of managing this mixture of emotions during entry and contracting is dealing with the dynamics of power. Power can swing back and forth between consultant and client, as they get in touch with what they might expose about themselves; worry about their competence and feel a need for containment. At entry, consultant and client are mutual and inescapable sources of anxiety for each other, as they negotiate around each other's perceptions of their needs, and their ability to bring their competences to bear in relation to them (Grueneisen & Izod, 2009). At the same time, both consultant and client have the possibility to offer containment to each other, to increase their potential to access their competence.

> Luke is concerned for his reputation as a newly independent consultant, as he contracts with a former colleague for some developmental work in which both consultant and client have expertise. The work is highly charged and political. The client feels a lone voice with his colleagues on this project, and Luke realises that he is there to validate his client's viewpoint, and as a guarantor of success. He cannot see how he can bring his own thinking to the table. Without the containment and confidence that both need to address what is at stake here, client and consultant risk getting into a collusive dynamic to "keep things safe". Neither of them will be able to work to best effect and the project risks mediocrity.

Scenario 1 expertise	Client requires/needs expertise	Consultant has expertise and wants to sell it
Scenario 2 expertise	Client has expertise and needs to access it	Consultant needs to elicit expertise in client
Scenario 3 containment	Client requires/needs containment	Consultant has capacity to contain
Scenario 4 containment	Consultant needs containment to work	Client has capacity to contain

Figure 5.5 Dynamics of expertise and containment in the process of hiring and being hired. Grueneisen & Izod, 2009, revised 2014.

Analytic Working with your competence and containment.

> Think about your own contracting activities and how you bring your competence:
>
> Do you notice your needs for containment? (Refer back to Chapter Two if you need some reminders about containment)
>
> Can you contain yourself, or do you need to access the resources of your colleagues, your client?
>
> Do you notice your client's needs for containment?
>
> What strategies do you use to access containment for your client?

5.4 Data and analysis and the dynamics of credibility and competition

Data compete for attention. Real world organisation analysis means working with some data at the expense of other data. We can think of the work of consulting and change as reality testing or "research". We find out what we can. We have gaps. We use models to help us think about our clients and their problems "as if" they exhibit the characteristics of our models. Models are metaphors. They are both essential and dangerous. We can be more and less conscious of the models we employ. The types of model of organisation and change we use will direct our attention to specific types of organisational problem and specific types of data. Other types of data and other problems will be not seen, or will be forgotten about, hidden, or ignored. Knowing your predilection for some models and your aversion to others is essential to resourceful practice.

Box 5.1 shows some well-known models or metaphors for understanding organisations popularised by Gareth Morgan (1986) and Manfred Kets de Vries & Danny Miller (1984). Which models of organisation do you prefer to inform your work and which do you never use?

Box 5.1 Models of organisation and where attention is directed

Organisation as **Machine**: performs explicit tasks as efficiently and effectively as possible. An organisation needs maintenance and can become obsolete.

Organisation as **Organism**: adapts to its environment with different challenges at each stage of its lifecycle. An organisation can be ill or healthy and only the fittest survive.

Organisation as **Brains**: meets unexpected challenges by evolving and self-organising its know-how. An organisation copes by learning and using its knowledge.

Organisation as **Culture**: creates small worlds for members and is imbued with values, norms, rituals, and roles. An organisation is self-perpetuating and can become trapped in its own history.

Organisation as **Political system**: struggles with self-interests and conflicts. An organisation is a collection of competing groups and priorities.

Organisation as **Psychic prison**: is trapped in obsessions, illusions, anxieties, and defence mechanisms. The organisation focuses on its internal needs.

Organisation as **Flux and transformation**: is constantly emerging and changing. An organisation is subject to complex and chaotic paradoxes and struggles to develop routines and structures.

Organisation as **Instrument of domination**: exploits people and the environment for questionable ends. An organisation seeks compliance and uses power to repress.

A **Paranoid Organisation** is always on the lookout for problems, distrusts newcomers and outsiders, and relates only to "friends" or "enemies".

A **Compulsive Organisation** operates through well-defined, rigid sets of rules, fears spontaneity and change, and relates to people as right or wrong.

A **Dramatic Organisation** acts on hunches and gut feelings. Everything is a drama and there is a belief of being different and "special".

A **Depressive Organisation** is very self-critical and carries the guilt of past failures. It prefers low risk, low investment strategies.

A **Schizoid Organisation** isolates itself, is afraid of being hurt and is suspicious and untrusting. It relates inconsistently and reactively towards outsiders.

Adapted from Morgan (1986) and Kets de Vries and Danny Miller (1984).

72   RESOURCE-FUL CONSULTING

Models make sense by representing only part of reality. We fill in the gaps. The model is not the thing it represents—it's a partial snap shot which we make sense of by drawing on our experience. The reality is often more weird than we can imagine.

Showing consultants some data (the picture of a woman's head, Picture A in Figure 5.6) they are asked to construct the whole picture, as if they are accessing data and offering an analysis in a consulting assignment. Their analyses usually include a woman on swing or a woman dancing with a partner. They are invariably surprised when the real picture is revealed (Picture B). If, instead of Picture A, some of the data had been excluded (the fish tail, for example, in Picture C), we would have a yet another picture or model of "the thing" we are dealing with.

Would showing our consultants different sets of data about the whole, maybe just the legs (Picture D) or the shadows (Picture E) have led to different analyses again?

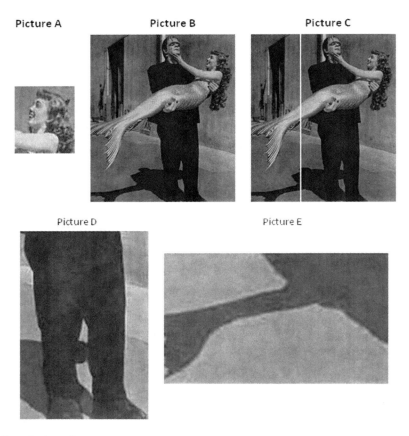

Figure 5.6 What do I see?
Accessed at http://www.bing.com/images/search?q=frankenstein+mermaid&FORM=IQFRBA&&id=8B9B7CB3065F986BA92A0D40B3BB4B308D346A67&selectedIndex=0#.

Analytic Data preoccupations.

Which sorts of data do you usually concentrate on and which do you exclude?

Where in your client system does your data come from—just the head, the legs, the shadows?

List some types of data that you always exclude and say why:

It's easy to fall into the trap of systematically ignoring data from particular aspects of the "whole thing" because:

- it doesn't fit with my analytic or intervention model:
- I don't understand/trust financial data, last year's data, experiential data
- I feel data from that department/those people/using that method is not credible.

We have a responsibility to look for the black swan (Taleb, 2007) that perturbs and disconfirms the models we use. The more preoccupied we are, the more difficult this is.

> Max was pleased to win a significant leadership training contract for a rapidly growing manufacturing company. In collecting data for a training needs analysis it became clear that middle managers had little trust in senior executives and the intervention would involve more than training. Max agrees a joint feedback meeting to both groups but instead of using middle managers own comments as data, he reinterprets them using less confronting language. Middle managers feel let down and the meeting does not go well. Max realises he had acted out the lack of trust and in doing so lost his credibility. In his anxiety about what might happen, he has failed to maintain a potential space to work in.

Identity is central to our capacity to make meaning. How we relate to data is inextricably linked to who I am and what I can recognise, in my inner world and outer worlds, as being valid. The psychic experience and the social experience and how they manifest are entirely related (Clarke, 2009). This involves:

- using imagination—the metaphors of organisation suggested above, and the ideas, images and fantasies that the work evokes in me
- having a capacity for empathy—thinking my way into colleagues' perspectives and understanding what is at stake for them

74   RESOURCE-FUL CONSULTING

- managing myself (regulation)—being aware of my patterns of identification, noticing what is triggered emotionally, and cognitively, being aware of when I feel confident in my perceptions and when I doubt them
- seeking meaning in my experience in relation to the task I am trying to do; what does my experience indicate or mean in this system?

> Jenni, an internal consultant working in retail, finds herself in competition with her client as to what the "real" nature of the problem is that she is brought in to help with. She is looking for the whole picture in her data gathering activities (as with Frankenstein and the Mermaid), so as to get to the truth.
>
> In the internal dynamics of the organisation, Jenni perceives herself as having less power and authority than her client, and so having a "truth" to present became an important signal to her client of her consulting competence. Jenni is reluctant to start to work with partial information, preferring to hold on to the fantasy that such a thing as complete data exists. To get out of this trap, she has to start letting herself deal with the immediate and grey data.

In consulting to change we are working not only with how we make sense of data, but how others are making sense of the data that they are noticing, with their own patterns of emotional resonances and identifications, and their own favourite models and theories. Unless we are able to work with partial pictures, to use our imaginations and curiosity to work with data, and check what we are encountering, we can run into a trap of thinking that there is only one system and only one meaning. When we restrict and impose limitations on whose data is valid, and what data is valid, then we start to lose the complexity of understanding necessary to analyse why organisations are stuck, and how to move them on.

> Amanda works in designing technical solutions in the knowledge industry. Her quick mind and analytic skills means that she often keeps ideas to herself, and progresses them independently. When she comes to collaborate with her organisational client and sponsor she finds herself easily dismissing their contribution—they clearly aren't on the same page as she is. Her over-reliance on her own sources of data and her own interpretation of them means that she struggles to keep her client system in mind and to conceptualise their needs for the project. When she meets with their perplexed responses, then she has a tendency to withdraw and give up, or be wildly ambitious. Either way it is a position of stuckness.

In this scenario, Amanda's over-reliance in her own way of doing things becomes competitive. She encounters a tension of "meaning constructed through me"—my identities, my context, my favourite ways of understanding, and "meaning constructed through others"—your identities, your context, your favourite ways of understanding. The challenge for her is to work at something much more mutual, a "meaning constructed with others" so that both client and consultant can offer some recognition to each other, and thereby some containment.

5.5 Interventions and the dynamics of risk and accountability

Many typologies of interventions are available (See Benne & Chin, 1985; Cummings & Worley, 2008; Heron, 2001; Schein, 1999 for some examples). These include explanatory, diagnostic, cathartic, human process, strategic, technological, structural, normative re-educative and power coercive interventions for achieving change. Each adopts a different perspective and choice of interventions based on their model-in-use of organisation and of change. Advice is also available about what a change strategy should include, implicitly or explicitly. Here is an example, using "client system" in place of "organisation".

> **Box 5.2 What a change strategy should include**
>
> 1. A model or metaphor of the client system and how it can change
> 2. Means to assess the current state of the client system and the preferred state (based on efficiency, effectiveness, renewal, health, trouble free, etc.)
> 3. A theory of intervention that indicates how to move the client system from the current state to the desired state (for example, the cycle of planned change, process consulting, lean manufacturing)
> 4. A definition of the role of consultant or change agent (as expert, trusted adviser, pertubator)
> 5. Some anticipation of social dynamics to be attended to (fear of the unknown, disruption of routine, loss of control, loss of face, loss of benefits, changes in organisation's compacts with employees, threats to identity or security, competition).
>
> Adapted from Weick and Quinn, 1999; Zell, 2003.

We use a psychoanalytic definition of intervention as *any* action taken by the consultant, knowingly or unknowingly that impacts the client system. Anything and everything we do, that relates to the client system, we think of as an intervention. That can include doing nothing! Learning how to regulate our emotions and manage anxieties so we can consider and choose how, when, and why to intervene is a constituent of resourceful consulting.

> Nina's way of coping with her preoccupations (of doing a good job, on time, whilst feeling she isn't really good enough) is to step up and take risks. Whilst colleagues and partners in her consulting firm take a more measured approach, Nina rushes in where angels fear to tread. She speaks up and takes responsibility when things are not going well with clients. She's the one who will present a half finished presentation and do a convincing job on the hoof. She longs to be taken more seriously and secure promotion to more seniority, but she can't see how. She enacts her inability to think more strategically, and her sense of lonely responsibility for what happens, both in her consulting practice and in her career management.

Nina moves around the model shown in Figure 5.7. She goes from trusting that it's a good idea to intervene, even though she is unclear about why or where she is going, to feeling depressed as reality kicks in and it is clear she is going nowhere and her interventions are not well thought through.

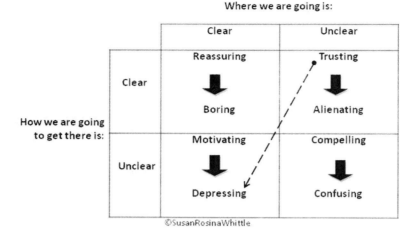

Figure 5.7 Taking risks with interventions.

What we imagine change looks like, and how we might get there, are frequent questions that clients ask. Are these responses familiar to you?

- reassurance—yes, I've done this before, and this is what happened
- trust—let's put our trust in the process and it will come out all right
- motivation—if we all work that bit harder/leaner we can get results
- compulsion—I'm really not sure what we have to do or how but whatever it is, we have to change!

How we relate to our clients, as they and we encounter our desires for and anxieties about change, means that we will find ourselves taking up a position about the kind of offer we can make. In Figure 5.7 each quadrant shows the emotional lure of intervening from a particular position of risk, as more or less is known about what to do and how to do it. Each intervention choice is an offer to the client system to engage in particular relational dynamics with the consultant: a relationship which is reassuring, trusting, motivating, compelling. Many consultancies niche their offers designed around these dynamics. But each has a flip side: the reassuring can become boring; the trusting alienating; the motivating depressing and the compelling confusing. The challenge for resourceful consulting is how to risk and account for all potential intervention relationships rather than being preoccupied with one or two of the more gratifying modes.

Getting caught up in definitive rather than provisional interventions is a consulting trap. As figure 5.7 suggests, the realities of consulting with strategies that over-rely on the personal appeal of the individuals involved, more than the hard resources of time, people, and money, can lead to boredom, depression and alienation. It can be a challenge to move into quadrant

4 at all. Acknowledging confusion (in the spirit of not-knowing outlined in Chapter Three) and letting go of some of the promised assurances of change can be difficult without adequate resources to draw on.

> Revati is seconded from a strategy role in an insurance company, to a strategy role in a public sector organisation, as part of a knowledge transfer initiative. From the beginning she feels a weight of responsibility to bring her skills to bear and make an impact, although how and where in the system she should attempt to bring influence is unclear. She has to find and make the role for herself. Revati is used to working in an organisation which works by adherence to regulation, and brings rational clarification to ambiguous situations. Her reassurance, "yes I've been here before, and this is what happened" isn't working for her as she finds herself facing a much messier and human environment involving multiple stakeholders. It's difficult to acknowledge that some of her desires for change stand little chance of being realised. She finds herself taking on more responsibility for change than is realistic, which in turn makes her more controlling. Her developmental challenge is to find a way to let go of her more controlling side, whilst still working with the responsibilities of her role.

To let go of control, Revati needs to embrace the plurality of the organisation she is now in, where different players (elected members, officers, service providers, members of the public and partnership agencies) all hold their views about any and everything. She needs to think specifically about who she is, how and where she includes herself (and consequently where she excludes herself), and how and where the system includes and excludes her. These political decisions, whether deliberate or unconscious, relate to Revati's "blind spots" in the Johari window (See Chapter One).

Any intervention for organisational change, such as a knowledge transfer initiative, can be conceptualised as a contested space, for multiple perspectives, agendas and interests to be played out (Hoggett, 2006). In this way, what might be a transformative and potential space for experimentation can also be a place where unequal social/professional/functional relations are worked on. Choices we make about who to involve and when, are visible, and can show where we position ourselves in relation to the powerful and marginal systems in organisations (and society) and the values that go with them. A large client system may require multiple interventions involving all the choices in Figure 5.7, simultaneously.

These are some of the practice issues we can encounter in deciding who to include and exclude in our interventions:

- Targeting (paying attention to the needs of specific groups may exclude other groups, for example, improved pay and terms and conditions for one group, may be detrimental for another)
- Impartiality and fairness, (if we allow you to do this, then we have to let everyone—but not everyone needs to!)
- Means/end phenomena (anything goes, as long as it works!)

And here are some ways to try to avoid being tripped up by not having a sense of the field of players that you might need to involve:

Box 5.3 Strategies for working on inclusion and exclusion

- Work from the consulting cycle to identity, classify (what kinds of interests do you need to hear about) and map out who you might need to include/exclude at any one point in the change cycle, in relation to the consultancy and change task.

- Watch for shifts in how organisational actors form, cluster, ally, and network, in relation to their positions over time.

- Stay open as to why you are including/excluding and manage any temptations to join alliances early in the consulting engagement. This involves noticing what our inner worlds might want to project onto specific interest groups that influence how we see them and our unwillingness to work with them.

5.6 Learning and regression and the dynamics of sustainability

Professional development is about learning new ways of thinking and behaving. Professional development is also about unlearning old, preoccupying ways, that compromise your presence and fail to support work with colleagues and clients.

Bateson speaks of knowing when learning has happened by the occurrence at time two of a different response from the response given at time one (Bateson, 1973). There is some change. There is no judgement about whether the change is desirable of not. We can learn bad things just as easily as good things. How quickly we learn and what we learn depends on our absorptive capacity. This is "[t]he ability to recognise the value of new external information, assimilate it and apply it to goals and objectives" (Cohen & Levinthal, 1990, p. 128).

Absorptive capacity is path dependent; what has happened in the past will influence what can happen in the future. If an individual or organisation has no history of changing, then their capacity to learn and change will be very limited. We know this from our consulting practice when young organisations, newly formed and used to assimilating new technologies and new recruits, often embrace change more readily than mature or family organisations that have changed very little for some time. In such organisations, learning and change can be threatening to self-image and identity and is rarely embarked on until there is some appreciation that existing practices and ways of being no longer work, for whatever reason.

Having worked in the sector for twenty years and now director of operations, Jack is used to fixing problems by having the answers. A recent merger has seen a new Board appointed with different ideas about how the company should be managed, including employee engagement and more open reporting of problems and failures. He doesn't know if he can cope with the upheaval and wonders whether to take redundancy. He never really liked the job anyway.

At this point, the choice is to engage in learning and change, with all the risks to identity and competence that entails, or to try and escape from or deny the need and stick to what you know, as Jack does, above. When the need is perceived as posing an intolerable risk (Hirschhorn, 1999), we might take refuge in maladaptive strategies (Crombie, 1993).

These are defences against the need to learn and change when we are struggling to cope with turbulent and highly unpredictable contexts (Emery & Trist, 1965). Turbulence fuels anxiety as cause and effect relationships, interests, and outcomes become uncertain. As feelings of helplessness and the fear of failure rise, we look for straightforward and reassuring choices. Six maladaptive strategies are described in Box 5.4.

Box 5.4 Six maladaptive strategies for coping with uncertainty

- A Strategy of Superficiality entails the lowering of emotional investment in work or relationships so that action is shaped by self interest or idiosyncratic whims.
- A Strategy of Segmentation refers to the loss of means-ends thinking so that action is governed more by hunch and opportunism than careful planning.
- A Strategy of Dissociation is characterised by a loss of common purpose and cynicism about what others and those in authority contribute to a task or relationship.
- A Strategy of Fundamentalism entails the assertion of an ideology or approach that renders complex situations amenable to simple remedies.
- A Strategy of Authoritarianism ensures certainty is regained through control and coercion.
- A Strategy of Evangelicism reassures and contains anxiety as individuals unite in causes, movements, and clubs.

Adapted from Crombie, 1993.

How might Jack make use of maladaptive strategies to cope with the uncertainty he feels? Maybe he will lower his emotional investment in his work or become more cynical of those in authority?

Conversely he might embrace the new regime and become evangelical. For those of us used to providing containment and certainty for others, it can be impossible to let go of control and learn something new that challenges the self.

Veronica, who has recently been appointed to an executive role in her company, now feels she has to act like an executive, rather than bring her executive qualities to bear on her role. In her view, she needs to provide a resilience embodied in a calm, knowing identity, even though the fast paced nature of the business means that exposure to new ideas, and organisational learning is ever present. While she doesn't present herself as authoritarian, the degree of certainty that dominates her mode of relating means that she is seen as being controlling. It is hard for her colleagues and her clients to admit to not understanding and making mistakes. Veronica needs to allow herself a more fallible presence, to recognise that she is part of this system of turbulence, so that she and her peers can start to address the rapid changes that are happening in her organisation and sector.

Another way of coping with the threat of change and the need for learning is to "carry on regardless". Trist first described the assumption of ordinariness as a psychological defence against a situation or experience one is not willing to confront (Trist et al., 1990). This defence enables us to perceive something in a containing way as "X with problems", rather than requiring us to think of something as a novel situation or experience with unknown dangers, potential threats to identity, and chances of failure.

Signposts that ordinariness might be at work as a defence include:

- the absence of any surprise of shock about what is happening
- a willingness to bend the rules and stretch protocols to make something work "as usual"
- and the making of statements or telling of stories about how "we usually do it this way".

> Ron faces the challenge of "we usually do it this way" as he begins work to develop a prestigious marketing programme for his consulting firm. The company already has a strong market presence and brand and his assignment works at the edge between introducing new ideas and disrupting the power of the brand, which needs to be sustained He'll need to watch out for multiple regressive dynamics as his colleagues and the firm's clients act out their preferred maladaptive strategies for coping with the loss of certainty about the firm's offer and fears of failure.

This is an example of how "organisational learning and organisational identity are related and interdependent" (Riise, 2009, p. 19). In this case, the identity portrayed through brand represents continuity and stability while learning represents change and instability. In his "backstage" work, Ron is in touch with a need to be credible, and for him that means that he has to work in depth on the assignment, so as to take the client into new territory for their products and for their brand. In doing so, he encounters the dynamics of "superficiality" of not disrupting the status quo, and thereby running the risk of stagnating. This is a point where it is easy to go off at a tangent, tinkering at the edges, shifting into idiosyncratic but more immediately rewarding activities, but which fail to keep the learning and the changes needed in mind.

Individuals and organisations have to make choices about what parts of their identity they need to stick to, and what requires change. Riise (2009, p. 27) describes four categories to help clarify these choices:

- How we perceive ourselves (identity)
- How we think others perceive us (image)
- How others perceive us (reputation)
- Continuous, coherent effort to strengthen reputation (brand).

Attending to these components invariably differentiates myself and my organisation from others. This in turn requires courage and willingness to be open to information coming from internal and external sources which have a bearing on how I perceive myself (my identity signifiers). This was the case for Aadit in Chapter Two, when his organisation suddenly grew, commanding greater resources, which then started to exclude him from prior networks. Noticing, listening to and valuing new sources of ideas and knowledge, is often hard. Think of how painful it is to read feedback forms and be open to what they offer, without being defensive or dismissive. Yet being closed down to this kind of learning can lead to a narcissistic complacency, as we protect our identities and image from change (Hatch & Schultz, 2002).

In the definition of learning offered earlier, time, and the difference between what we do at one time, and what we do at another, is the key variable.

> Mart designed a series of educational events with an organisation that is facing difficulties in retaining its staff. They are reluctant to carry out exit interviews and prefer to work with their impressions of why people leave rather than seeking out data. Mart's preference for long term interventions seems well suited to this client's specific needs. Yet each time that Mart arrives for a session, he finds himself going over the same ground, reminding people of what they are there for, and what they are trying to achieve. He feels that there is no memory held of the work and that he is taking up a role to provide continuity. Although each session seems productive, he feels he and they are back where they started each time. This is an old organisation, priding itself on its history and respecting the way it does things, yet it seems to suffer from amnesia. Mart needs to find a new way to bring himself to this client. Relying on his old repertoire, which works so well for many of his clients, is getting in the way of his openness to the challenge of new learning. He is bringing something that belongs to his past, rather than his present.

Analytic Past the sell-by date.

How long it is since you introduced new sources, methods, designs, into your consulting practice?

How would you assess your absorptive capacity?

Do you have favourite models and interventions? Imagine if someone told you that these could not be used in your next assignment. Are you likely to employ any maladaptive strategies?

What would you need to do to renew your repertoire?

5.7 Evaluation and exit and the dynamics of endings and loss

Evaluations, exits and endings, can be times in the consulting cycle when poorly contracted work goes awry and unfinished business (those buried issues, compromises, and unresolved conflicts) come to the fore. There may be an air of the last-chance-saloon or of opportunities lost for consultant and/or client as projects end and evaluations begin. Block (2000) offers a list of factors that inform our judgements about how we evaluate our consulting work on exit and later.

Box 5.5 Evaluating consulting work

1. Aspirations compared to realities. The client or the consultant was:
   - Underwhelmed
   - Satisfied
   - Ecstatic, best thing ever

2. Contracted process compared to actual process in terms of:
   - Time
   - Cost
   - Fun
   - Pain

3. Ethics compared to experiences. The work:
   - Was affirming or negating of identities (self, professional, organisational)
   - Used developmental or regressive interventions and outcomes
   - deployed ethical or compromising practices.

Adapted from Block (2000).

Analytic Evaluating your work.

> Use Block's three headings and list how you evaluate your last two or three work assignments.

We looked earlier in this Chapter at the extent to which learning and regression are constant features in organisational change, a weaving back and forth between exposure to new ideas, acting on those ideas, and stepping back from them as they cease to be relevant. Change isn't continuous and so attempts to evaluate what has changed have to bear in mind what is still changing and what remains unchangeable.

Kirkpatrick's (1994) model of programme evaluation continues to offer a structure to examine the way individuals learn, and how their learning makes its way into organisational life. He suggests four levels for assessment:

- Level One—Reaction—the thoughts and feelings of the moment
- Level Two—Learning—usually quantifiable (a before and after comparison) and tending to be technical rather than attitudinal learning
- Level Three—Behavioural change—considers implementation and application of learning
- Level Four—Organisational performance—considers extent to which change is embedded in behaviours and cultures of organisation, and often is the basis for return-on-investment analyses.

Our interest is in looking at how we have been able to help consultants and change agents to intervene to effect change with their clients and in their organisations. Using Kirkpatrick as a starting point, the model below suggests levels of change that we can gather data about, utilising some of the resources and concepts of our approach.

Box 5.6 Assessing levels of change: perspectives from a resource-ful approach

Level of change	Data to note for evaluation	Time dimension
Cognitive	How have the models and theories I have worked with influenced the client's capacities to conceptualise and talk about their situation? What shifts do I notice in the use of language and narratives? (relates to Kirkpatrick's level two)	Is the change temporary? How do I know if it will sustain?
Behavioural	How has the client system (and its individual or group players) shifted in relation to their preferred routines and responses? What new repertoires of behaviour are possible and what outputs start to be visible? (relates to Kirkpatrick's level three)	Is the change temporary? How do I know if it will sustain?
Emotional	Has it been possible to disentangle some of the emotions that keep individuals and system in stuck positions? What new "recognitions" are possible for individuals and systems?	Is the change temporary? How do I know if it will sustain?
Structural—political	What shifts and redistributions of power, resources, opportunities, rewards, energies, constraints are observable?	Is the change temporary? How do I know if it will sustain?

Mart (whose consultation to the organisation struggling with its memory is described in the preceding vignette), works with a hypothesis that the organisation is facing changes in its external environment which it is reluctant to face. They recognise that they are late to embrace new technologies, online services in particular. He attempts to focus on what is happening in the present, as much as what happened in the past with the intention of weaving new routines into the old. Over time, he and they notice that: the managers decide to meet more frequently, which is seen by staff as them taking up a more positive leadership role; that his workshops are better attended, and people arrive on time and are more willing to share their ideas. He notices that he also is coming to the sessions willing to let go of his role of holding the continuity and facing whatever confusion arises as a consequence. He holds doubts about whether this change can sustain without his intervention, and he finds himself reluctant to take that risk on their behalf.

In this situation Mart is not only coming up against short/long term consulting issues, but the difficulty of when and how to end the work, what is good enough change, and whose responsibility is it to sustain it?

Analytic Assessing levels of change.

> Using the levels of change in Box 5.6 above:
>
> What types of data do you notice that you are looking at as consulting projects end: are they cognitive, behavioural, emotional, political/structural?
>
> Does this reveal anything to you about where you are trying to impact the system? Is any level absent or overly present?
>
> Do you need to realign your evaluations to take notice of where and how change might be happening that you might not be aware of?
>
> What conversations can you have with yourself and your client that might help you to decide when to end the work and why?

Deciding when and how to end work with a client may not be within our gift. The unexpected happens, and consulting rugs can be pulled from beneath our feet. We have found that attachment patterns (Bowlby, 1969) offer a framework that can be particularly helpful in working with evaluation and ending phases with a client.

Attachment theory appeals to us in our professional development work. We all demonstrate attachment patterns. These embody the quality of attentiveness we have experienced in our early relationships and the expectations we build up as to whether our needs are likely to be noticed and met or not. Early interactions with caregivers create patterns in our emotional range and influence the extent to which we involve others to help us and can make ourselves emotionally available to others. These patterns of attachment come to the fore as learned responses when we need to avoid threat, or seek comfort. Do I have people I usually turn to and talk things over or ask for help or do I feel I have to sort things myself?, In adult life we can think of attachment patterns as default settings for how much safety and risk we seek, for whether we have preferences for being alone or in the company of others, for experimentation or for staying with the tried and trusted. They form a regulation process for how we manage ourselves in times of stress and discomfort, how we view ourselves and others. Behaviours arising from our attachment patterns can be easily evoked in the workplace, where attachment to place and routine develops, and authority figures can evoke earlier relationships with parental figures.

Bowlby's original work suggests three attachment patterns:

- Secure attachment—arises from early experiences of being related to by a sensitive, available, attentive parental figure, and is evidenced in individuals with a basically high self-esteem, with capacity to empathise with and approach others.

- Anxious (ambivalent) attachment—arises from early experiences of uncertainty in relations to attachment figures—not knowing if the parent will be available, responsive, or helpful, together with a fear of abandonment. This is evidenced by clinging and worried behaviours.
- Anxious (avoidant) attachment—arises from early experiences of not feeling understood, not having feelings confirmed or perhaps having approaches rebuffed. Those of us with this attachment pattern can seem unapproachable and disinterested in others.

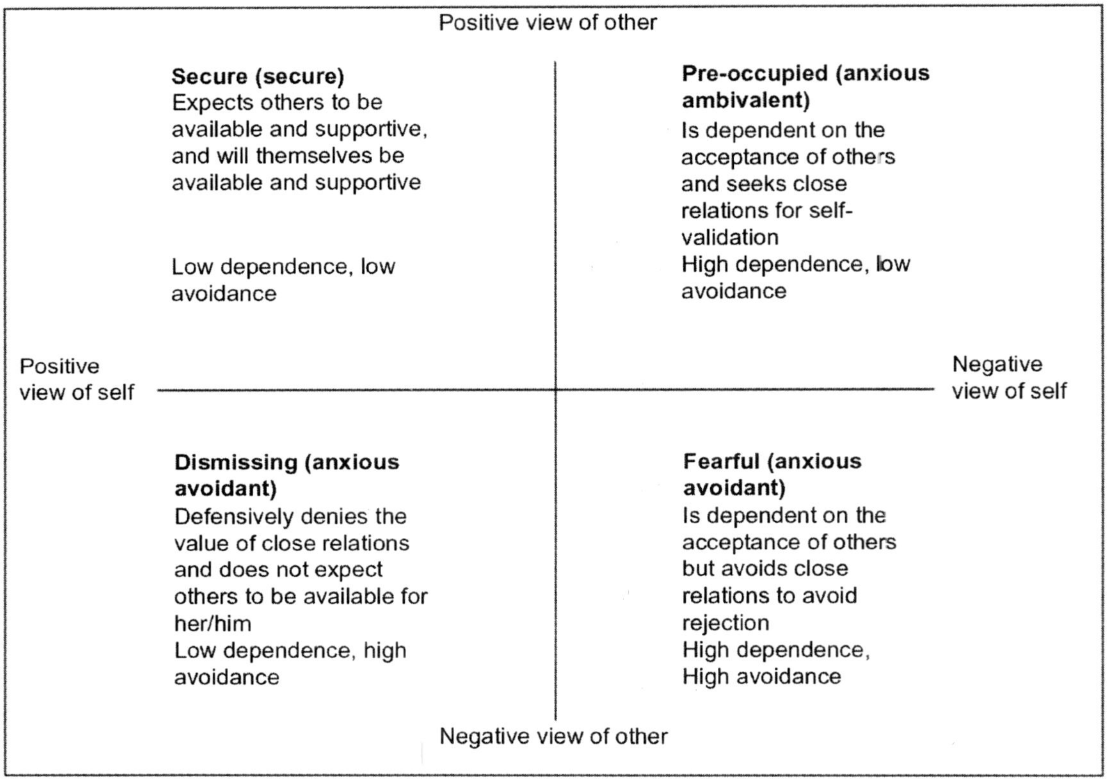

	Positive view of other	
Positive view of self	**Secure (secure)** Expects others to be available and supportive, and will themselves be available and supportive Low dependence, low avoidance	**Pre-occupied (anxious ambivalent)** Is dependent on the acceptance of others and seeks close relations for self-validation High dependence, low avoidance
Negative view of self	**Dismissing (anxious avoidant)** Defensively denies the value of close relations and does not expect others to be available for her/him Low dependence, high avoidance	**Fearful (anxious avoidant)** Is dependent on the acceptance of others but avoids close relations to avoid rejection High dependence, High avoidance
	Negative view of other	

Figure 5.8 Attachment patterns.
Adapted from Bartholomew & Horowitz, 1991.

Bartholomew & Horowitz (1991) have developed this work to consider adult attachment behaviours including the variables of dependency on, or avoidance of others, and positive and negative views of self and other.

> Raoul notices that he can never get his coaching clients to come to their last session. It's always difficult for them to get a date in the diary, and he doesn't like to push them, so his work tends to fizzle out rather than come to an end. He realises that this is a way in which he avoids the emotional aspect of loss which comes with ending an assignment. He can also keep a fantasy alive that the assignment is still continuing, and therefore that he doesn't need to deal with evaluating his own work.

> Jane easily offers support to her team colleagues and expects that her ideas will be sought out. She also takes her consulting role seriously, welcomes feedback and takes care that what she offers is relevant and developmental. Yet Jane struggles to get a similar level of support from her boss and feels pushed away whenever she asks for his opinions. She thinks she is encountered as needy and unable to work independently.

These differences in attachment patterns can play out in evaluation activities, both in the extent to which I and my clients can find sufficient common ground to begin a conversation and to be willing to hear each other's feedback. The capacity to take on new information (as we discussed in learning and regression) is significantly impacted by our own patterns, when we, as consultants and clients, may be looking for reassurances from each other, or want to avoid some painful realities.

Analytic Assessing attachment patterns when working with evaluations and endings.

> Using the grid above in figure 5.8:
>
> Can you identify your own attachment patterns? You can expect to have a dominant pattern as your default, but also for aspects of all four to come into effect at different times.
>
> How does this influence the way you go about evaluating your work with a client?
>
> How does this influence the way you go about ending your work with a client?
>
> What might you notice about your client's attachment patterns in these situations?
>
> Explore with a colleague the way that different attachment patterns interact, for instance, my dismissive pattern interacts with your fearful pattern.

5.8 Summary proposition

How you think of yourself, present yourself, and relate to others, shapes your authority, defines your credibility, governs your access to data, and your opportunities to influence and lead change.

We will work on how I can use my identity and presence as resources in my consulting work in Chapter Six—Change.

CHAPTER SIX

Change: developing resource-ful practice

Karen Izod and Susan Rosina Whittle

6.1 Mind the gap between knowing and doing

There is a huge gap between knowing what to do and knowing how to do it. As a result, many organisational change initiatives fail after a short time. The good intentions formulated in training and development programmes are not sustained. Reading this book will not make you a more resourceful consultant. You need to act; run some experiments; risk doing different things and doings things differently; evaluate the impact and act again.

This chapter focusses on how we can reorganise ourselves for work. Much as we might decide to makeover a room, bringing in new furniture, restyling, and reorienting the room for a different look or feel, then this is about how you can make some changes to the way that you combine aspects of your identity and presence to reorganise and change your practice.

In this chapter you will find:

- Ideas about how we work with change
- Effecting change with presence preoccupations
- Effecting change with identity preoccupations.

The term "winging it" has mixed meaning: it can imply getting away with something, faking it, but also being improvisational, trying something out just in time. It comes from the idea of learning your lines in the theatre wings, that space that is in between the front and the back stage. This is where we located role, available in the wings—as props to one's identity and presence, there for the picking and choosing in the moment. Choosing where and how to experiment with change brings its own dilemmas. Do you try something new for the first time with your client, or do you experiment in a safe space with colleagues? Do you only bring tried and tested techniques to your client, and then risk the loss of spontaneity? These are some of the aspects of presence that Susan Rosina Whittle worked with earlier in Chapter Three.

6.2 A note about how we work with change and our understanding of change

We are talking here about making changes to the way we think about things and the way that we do things that constitute our professional practice. The primary tool that we make use of is "potential space" with its combination of play, transitional phenomena, cultural experience and analytic activity (Ogden, 1992, p. 203) to create the platform to experiment with formulations of our Identity and Presence, and to access our creativity.

Change happens in the present, not the past or the future. Change is about trying things out in the "now", in a spirit of experimentation. That doesn't mean to say that how we did things in the past has to be rejected, forgotten, or denigrated. Even when we welcome change, it can evoke a sense of loss for the way that we have habitually done things, and with loss can come a loss of meaning (Marris, 1982). This is how, for instance, I can welcome starting a new job, welcome the kinds of tasks that it involves, look forward to trying out new skills, but yet feel so disoriented when I have to learn new things. We get separated, dislocated from our thinking at a point where some long-held belief or way of doing something no longer seems valid. We may have to modify or give up a view of ourselves that we find attractive, and have grown attached to in order to shake free from our preoccupations.

Our intention in working with professional development is to find new ways to relate to these patterns, to reorganise ourselves in relation to them, rather than to disregard or dismiss the already known, and the already tried. This means weaving new patterns into the fabric of our practice by being open to the gap afforded between reality and fantasy through potential space. This "ongoing process of helping people to recognise, evaluate and change patterns: patterns of action, thought and habitual behaviour" is a good enough description of our approach to professional development (Alder, 2010, p. 4). It is about being present in this moment, rather than living in the past or escaping into the future. We describe more about our approach to change in the Appendix.

6.3 Effecting change with presence preoccupations

We revisit those preoccupations with authority that shape presence (confidence, competition, and control) and offer ways to start changing these preoccupations into assets to craft a more resourceful presence.

6.3.1 Confidence

The self-confident change practitioner is someone who trusts themselves to behave appropriately, to help their client, and to complete their assignment. Self-confidence comes from knowing that whatever the situation, you will know what to do. But a resourceful practitioner is

NOT confident that in any situation they know what to do. You can't work with what you don't know—but you need to be confident about not knowing. A resourceful practitioner is confident in knowing how to contain the anxieties evoked by not knowing.

This is known as "negative capability". Negative capability is the advanced ability of a person to tolerate uncertainty. This does not mean the passive uncertainty associated with ignorance or general insecurity but the active uncertainty that is to do with being without a template and yet being able to tolerate, or even relish, a sense of feeling lost. Negative capability involves purposely submitting to being unsettled by a person, or situation, and embracing the feelings and possibilities that emerge. (Voller, 2010).

That purpose is to "use emotion as information for understanding the work …" (French, 2000, p. 1) Too little confidence and we can be overwhelmed by the anxiety of not knowing. Over confidence shuts out uncertainty and anxiety and leaves no space for not knowing. The anxiety of not knowing which cannot be worked with or used as a source of data can be dispersed into explanations or emotional and physical reactions. Explaining away what we do not know fills the potential space for discovering something new. Dispersal into emotional or physical reactions is acting out, a way of closing off what we do not want to acknowledge (Bion, 1999) (See Chapter One, Potential space.) How is the preoccupation of having too little confidence or being over confident addressed as a professional development issue? The challenge is (a) to work with what you do know, by analysing how you feel as well as what you think, and (b) to find ways to tolerate the uncertainty of what you don't know. This frees up attention to finding out what you need to know to intervene rather than what stops you from intervening, what you can do rather than what you cannot do. The bystander figure is helpful to those wanting to change their preoccupation with too little confidence.

6.3.1a The bystander

Too little confidence can evoke withdrawal and inaction whereby the consultant or change agent fails to intervene and takes on the status of bystander. A harrowing example of potential change agents failing to intervene is offered in the case of James Bulger, a three-year-old child abducted in a busy UK shopping centre by two young boys and eventually murdered (Levine, 1999). CCTV shows James protesting, crying as he is pulled along through the shopping centre and outside. Why did no one intervene to find out why the child was so distressed or what the boys were doing with him? The explanation offered by many shoppers was that they thought James and his abductors were siblings, all members of the same family. Shoppers, as strangers, had no authority to intervene. Rather than working with their felt anxiety as data about what is happening in front of their eyes, shoppers chose to explain away the anxiety of not knowing what to do in this scenario. Making sense of what they saw as "a family matter" legitimated their non-intervention.

Most of us become adept at dispersing the anxiety of not knowing into explanations that legitimate taking a bystander position. The not knowing often comes out of a felt existential risk to the self. Unable to tolerate the uncertainty of not knowing what to do, explanations offer rationales about why I shouldn't say this or do that. Explanations keep me safe, even if I don't much like the "me" implied by the explanation. Recognising when I am taking a bystander position offers insights into which situations and experiences evoke anxiety for me such that I choose to withdraw or fail to act.

Work through the questions in the below analytic and see what you discover about your own negative capability.

Analytic The bystander.

> Think of one or two work situations where you regret not intervening (either through speaking or taking action).
>
> At the time, what explanation came to mind that enabled you to take up a bystander position?
>
> What feelings are evoked now, when you think back about what you didn't say or didn't do?
>
> What could you have done to authorise yourself to risk an intervention in that situation?
>
> Can you name the risk you felt?

6.3.1b The trekker

At other times and in other situations, or indeed as a default, over confidence can be a practice-preoccupation also. Over confidence undermines authority and shapes presence in unhelpful ways, just as much as a lack of confidence. Going where angels fear to tread, with certainty, can be foolhardy and self serving, rather than designed to help the client. Star-trekkers "boldy go" when they really need to refrain from intervening. Taking old ladies across the road whether they want to go or not might make you feel good but not the old lady. Have there been instances recently in your professional life where you have regretted intervening (saying what you said or doing what you did) when it would have been better to not? If so, see if you can answer the questions in the analytic below.

Analytic Star-trekking.

> **Think of one or two work situations where you regret intervening.**
>
> **At the time, what explanation(s) came to mind that enabled you to intervene in this way?**
>
> **What feelings are evoked now, when you think back about what you said or did?**
>
> **What could you have done to authorise yourself to risk not intervening in those situations?**
>
> **Can you name the risk you felt?**

Unfortunately, acknowledgement and explanation do not change anything! Understanding why something is like this or that doesn't help on its own. Indeed, a well-rehearsed explanation can hinder change by perpetuating ways of thinking and doing that maintain anxiety-avoiding behaviours. Change requires different actions and that depends on having different understandings of what is happening and what might happen. Helping practitioners to draw new inferences about what's happening is a powerful way to develop negative capability and open new options for intervening.

6.3.1c Drawing inferences

An inference is "a guess that you make or an opinion that you form based on the information that you have" (sourced from Cambridge Dictionaries Online). When we infer something, we relate to the information we have as true and to the assumptions we make as logical. Here is an example:

INFORMATION: My client is late for a meeting.
INFERENCE: My client no longer wants to work with me.

If the information is not true or if the assumptions made are not logical, the inference drawn will be inaccurate. This seems straight-forward and easy to test. The problem is that assumptions are rarely articulated explicitly. They lie buried in the inference. Take the above example.

Analytic Inferences.

- Write down other inferences that could be drawn from the information about my client being late for a meeting.

- What are the assumptions that make each inference a logical conclusion?

- Think what additional information you might look for to validate each inference.

- What are the assumptions leading to the inference "My client no longer wants to work with me?"

- How can the validity of this inference be tested?

An inaccurate inference is called a fallacy. This happens when:

1. A logical conclusion drawn from false data leads to a false inference.
2. An illogical conclusion drawn from true data leads to a false inference.

Box 6.1 shows an example of each.

Box 6.1 Two types of fallacy when drawing inferences	
1. All consultants have lots of confidence in themselves. (False)	1. Consultants have anxieties about "not knowing". (True)
2. I am not confident in myself. (True)	2. Children have anxieties about "not knowing" (True)
3. Therefore, I can't be a competent consultant. (False)	3. Therefore, consultants are children. (False)

A useful tool to make explicit the way inferences are drawn is the "ladder of inference". Originally developed by Chris Argyris (1992), there are several versions available that are very accessible. See for example Senge, 1994. http://www.systems-thinking.org/loi/loi.htm.

The process of drawing inference from experience is often shown as a ladder to emphasise how steps in the process follow on from each other logically. Here's an example of me (Susan) at a conference, to show the ladder of inference at work.

1. From my ongoing "real life experiences".
2. I select "data" that attracts my attention. (Maybe it's who is speaking. Maybe it's the traffic noise outside.)
3. To the data I have selected and through my experiences in the moment, I:
   a. "Affix meaning" (Speaker X is great. I can hear her above the traffic noise. Speaker Y is terrible. She can't even talk above the traffic noise.)
   b. Develop "assumptions" (A good consultant can always make themselves heard.)
   c. and come to "conclusions". (Speaker X must be a great consultant. Speaker Y is clearly incompetent.)
4. Finally, I develop "beliefs". (It's their job for speakers to make their knowledge available to me. If these consultants can't be bothered, they can't be saying anything that's useful to me.)
5. Beliefs then form the basis of my "actions" (I won't waste my time and contact Speaker Y again).
6. These in turn create further data and experiences.

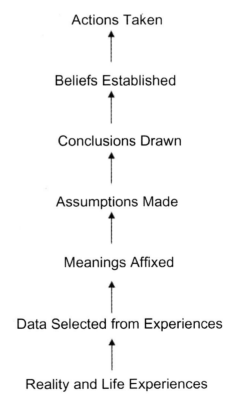

Figure 6.1 Ladder of inference.

96 RESOURCE-FUL CONSULTING

The problem with inference is that beliefs and assumptions can short circuit this process and start to drive the data I select and the meanings I affix to them (see Figure 6.2). Being aware of how your beliefs and assumptions lead to fallacies and inaccurate conclusions can help you tell different stories about yourself, your confidence, and your work.

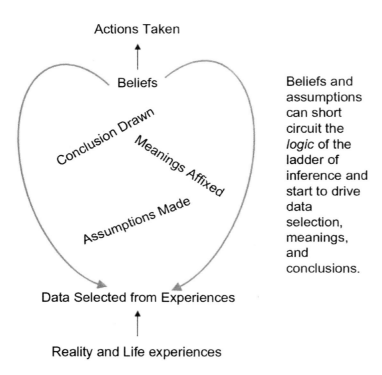

Figure 6.2 Drawing inferences.

Analytic Drawing inferences.

Look at Figure 6.2 and try this exercise to catch a glimpse of the beliefs governing your own data selection and interpretation.

Locate a buddy who has ten minutes to spare, or a colleague, friend or family member. Think of someone you both know and each of you write down what you know about this person and what you think of them.

Share conclusions about the person, noticing:
- What data you each select.
- The meanings each of you affix to the data and the person.

Now have a conversation about:
- The assumptions you each made.
- The beliefs you each hold about people in relation to this person.

What have you learned about the inferences you make?

6.3.2 Competition

Competition is natural and can be helpful in providing energy and motivation to act and achieve desired outcomes. Competition is also a great leveller, removing distinctions based on history, status or privilege, and bringing into stark relief comparisons, evaluation, and judgement about what's happening now. Judgement is what makes competition such a powerful preoccupation for so many consultants and change leaders. Karen Horney (1950) used the term "hyper-competitiveness" to describe someone who needs to win all the time in order to prove their self-worth. Do you know someone who will turn anything and everything into a competition? After some years, I refused to play board games at Christmas with a relative because he was deadly serious in his quest to win. He couldn't have fun, and neither could we. Perhaps that's you? The possibility of losing didn't fit his sense of himself, his idealised self, with whom he was in perpetual competition.

Feelings of self-worth are learned, as we encounter the judgements of our parents and authority figures. Karen Horney spoke of how the "tyranny of the shoulds" is applied to real life experiences and achievements which invariably fail to meet the standards of the idealised self (Horney, 1950). In these situations, the real life or true self can be despised. Consequently, the hypercompetitive individual either competes even harder to realise her ideal, or withdraws to avoid the possibility of failing to live up to this normative, internal voice. Here, the part of myself that fails to meet my idealised expectations might be projected onto others, who are in turn despised (See Chapter Two).

We expect competition to be a practice preoccupation for change professionals when there is:

- A contest, conscious or unconscious, to secure what are believed to be scarce resources, such as an attribute or characteristic, or a position in a social, economic or psychological ranking; the well known scenario "this town ain't big enough for both of us".
- A felt need to defend against feelings of inferiority and lack of self-worth, such as when you know you are not going to be picked for the football team.

Competition can take many forms. We can see competition preoccupations at work as:

- A contest over who should take what role with the client: persecutor, victim, or rescuer;[1] expert, or buddy; good cop, or bad cop.
- A device to enhance or protect my status in a group, for example, by showing my contempt for "menial" tasks or an inept client, or aligning myself with opinion leaders.
- A felt need to be judged as "more" or "less" of something than you are. In behavioural terms, this might mean being judged as more competent, more creative, more confused, or more expensive than you; or to be less afraid, less in need of work, or less willing to help than you.

Being preoccupied runs the risk of my becoming a slave to competition or of being afraid of competition. Often, those whose behaviour is very competitive are unaware of their preoccupation. It's a way of life where all potential space becomes about winning, whatever that means, or of finding ways to avoid the contest. Winning does not always mean achieving the task or objective, as long as the idealised self is served (Levine, 2001). This absence of awareness makes a preoccupation with competition difficult to address on our own. Our experience is that finding ways to access feedback is the most effective intervention.

Stop the competing long enough to hear some feedback

Feedback is not usually of interest to those of us preoccupied with competition. We can ignore it because our most important judge is ourselves. We have learned to defend ourselves with varying degrees of success, against negative and hurtful comments from others, by projecting those devalued parts of ourselves onto them.

Feedback is an exchange between people which can be planned or unplanned. It is an intervention designed to influence what's happening by offering data about:

- Working relationships
  - We worked really well together today
  - I wish we didn't clash so much over a small thing like that

- Needs and experiences
    - I can't work like that
    - I need more time than you
- Hopes and disappointments
    - I couldn't believe what you said in there
- Achievements and failures
    - How can we avoid/repeat this in the future?

If someone keeps looking at their watch whilst talking to you, that's feedback. Quite what the feedback is will need to be deciphered but it is likely to be something along the lines of

"Hurry up. I don't want to be here much longer with you".

Whilst there might be a clause in brackets after this statement ("even though I want to") the feedback still stands.

Is there someone you would feel able to say this to and anyone you would feel unable to say it to?

Embedded within feedback are rules about:

- What can and what cannot be discussed between people or "brought into the room".
- Anticipated and enacted responsibilities (who does what, how, when).
- Roles, resources and commitments about time, people, money, and risks.
- Ground rules on confidentiality and information sharing and what is acceptable and unacceptable behaviour.
- What the feedback means and what to do about it (See Block, 2000).

These rules are rarely if ever discussed. They remain tacit until someone breaks them and collaboration changes to competition (Walsh & Whittle, 2009).

Analytic Data selection and interpretation.

> Think of people you work with.
>
> Is there anyone you don't have much time for, who you feel doesn't contribute much or gets in the way because of their (lack of) skills or knowledge or because of their attitude or personal characteristics?
>
> What irritates you about them? Make a list.
>
> Now think of people you could socialise with if you could tolerate their ....
>
> Which words would you put in here? Write them down, too.
>
> Find someone you value and ask them about the list you have made and the words you wrote down. Do they relate to you at all and how others encounter you? Can you recognise yourself in these words?
>
> If you don't have access to talk to someone informally, consider contracting for a session or two with a shadow consultant.

6.3.2a Inquiry or advocacy

Here is another way you can analyse how competition shapes your presence. Developed from work by Chris Argyris and others,[2] the advocacy and inquiry matrix differentiates exchanges between people which are dominated by inquiry and those where advocacy prevails. An adapted version is shown in Figure 6.3.

Any exchange can be pulled away from mutual engagement if one or other party engages predominantly in questioning the other or (taking an inquiry mode) dismissing the other (taking

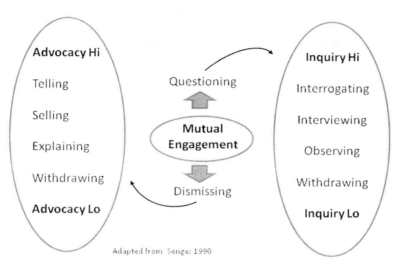

Figure 6.3 Inquiry and advocacy modes.

an advocacy mode.) Those of us preoccupied with competition tend to find ourselves taking up an advocacy rather than an inquiry mode in our exchanges with others. We are encountered as telling and selling, rather than interviewing and observing, or if we are preoccupied with avoiding competition, as withdrawing. The challenge is how to move from a presence in which advocacy is excessively present to one that includes more inquiry. Box 6.2 offers some suggestions.

Box 6.2 Advocacy > Inquiry

- Be clear and explicit about the thinking informing what you say and do.
  (Write down why you are advocating this or that and subject it to critique. Discuss the data and rationale for whatever you are advocating with whomever you are working with.)

- Invite others to explore your views and proposals
  (Ask others whether they see any problems with or gaps in what you are advocating.)

- Encourage others to provide different views, rationales, and proposals to the ones you advocate.
  (Actively search for alternatives and create a potential space to help others speak up.)

- Listen to those you feel most dismissive of.
  (Actively inquire about their views and proposals and try them out.)

The key to balancing advocacy and inquiry is noticing which mode you are in. It's not unknown for competition to be focused on who asks the most questions!

102   RESOURCE-FUL CONSULTING

6.3.3 Control

It is fashionable now, when designing organisations and describing your management philosophy, to speak about trust rather than control. Awareness of the power of social capital, of networks, and social media has pushed psychological contracting, relational decision-making and trust into the spot light. The approach now is to take the horse to water and hope that it drinks. This means we sometimes avoid talking about control, as if it belongs to another era, like communism or other forms of hierarchy. As a result, it is more difficult for those of us with a preoccupation for control to acknowledge that and "come out", even to ourselves.

Two frequently encountered preoccupations with control, that can shape authority and compromise a resourceful presence, are:

- the felt need to be in control—of my emotions, of others, of tasks, of process, etc., etc.
- the felt need to avoid responsibility for controlling—what happens, what others think or feel, for outcomes, for equity, for success, etc., etc.

You may find it helpful to remind yourself about a preoccupation with control in Chapter Three. Trust, or the lack of trust, can play a big part in understanding both these preoccupations. Earlier in this chapter, we spoke about negative capability as the "ability of a person to tolerate uncertainty … and purposefully submit to being unsettled" (p. 91). This implies that I can contain myself and regulate my emotions enough to work with uncertainty and not knowing. These are prerequisites for consulting to change.

If I don't trust that I can regulate my emotions or tolerate the uncertainty of what others do, I may overcompensate and either withdraw from all responsibility or put in places practices and routines to put me in control. Here are a few examples of typical routines used by those with a preoccupation with control:

- Trying to design out the unexpected (from a meeting, a report, a workshop, a working relationship) by specifying the agenda, the process, the contributors.
- Taking up the role of leader or expert and speaking with assumed authority.
- Working with those that I trust to collaborate and comply with me and excluding those I don't.
- Putting in place water-tight contingencies and prescriptions "just in case" something does not go according to plan.
- Expressing few opinions and waiting for others to make suggestions or take actions.
- Agreeing with the person leading the event or group at the time, even if this means changing "sides" over and over again.

A felt need for control may develop from my assumption that I know what to do and that I can trust no-one to do as good a job as I can. I have the right understanding of the problem, the skills, awareness of context, experience, or whatever and you do not. Blind certainty comes from an intolerance to multiple ways of understanding and relating to change, to people, to tasks. Quite a handicap for consulting! The book, and now the film, *Minority Report* (Dick, 1956) raises the notion of control through an assumption of privileged knowledge to a societal level.

6.3.3a Strategies for control

How can I loosen my conviction that, if don't take control, disaster looms? As with competition, the first step is to acknowledge that there are many forms of control and some are more palatable than others. Think about how to diagnose a problem, lead a group, or authorise an intervention and the options for controlling these activities.

Henry Mintzberg (1991) offered a typology of control mechanisms. These are shown in Box 6.3.

Box 6.3 Control mechanisms

- **Mutual adjustment**, where control is exercised through the here-and-now process of negotiated action and reaction, between two or more people. "We can work it out".
- **Direct supervision**, in which control is achieved by one person issuing orders and instructions to others or guiding them in what to do by example. "Follow me and do it this way."
- **Standardisation of outputs**, where control is exercised by specifying and then assessing the outputs or results achieved, such as profit, time, or client satisfaction, not how they are achieved. "This report has to be with the client by 9 a.m."
- **Standardisation of work** processes does focus on how people work on tasks or relate to clients and achieves control by specifying the way people way work and tasks are done. "We need to work more slowly in this phase to help the client think through the possibilities."
- **Standardisation of skills** again focusses on how work is done but this time control is achieved through inputs to the work process, such as individual training and development and the acquisition/deployment of appropriate attitudes and knowledge. "If Jane, Tim and Claire are brought into the team, we'll have the right talent mix."
- **Standardisation of culture or mission** whereby control is achieved by everyone buying into a shared purpose or sense of organisational identity. "It's up to us. We know what to do."

Analytic Working on control mechanisms.

Can you spot your own preferences?

List the mechanisms you tend to use most frequently.

What would you say are the pros and cons of these for the types of work you do?

Are you uncomfortable or avoidant of any mechanisms?

Different approaches to control and the choice of mechanisms used come out of different views about:

- what counts as information and
- how to understand and explain what's happening in my work.

Thinking of consulting and change as detective work can make these different approaches to control clearer. If we think of some well-known detectives, they employ very different practices to establish what happened and to understand a crime scene. They have specific routines to control the way they work (adapted from Thorpe & Moscorola, 1991).

- **Poirot** is the armchair detective, constructing hypotheses about what could have happened, testing them against logic and deducing their validity. He thinks through what could and should happen, creates a model or plan, and then executes it.
- **Wallander's** approach is to enter into the criminal's mind and understand his way of thinking by visiting where he lives, who he associates with, and what his past reveals. Empathising and standing in the shoes of others gives Wallander insights to anticipate the criminal's behaviour.
- **James Bond's** approach is try it and see! He is quick witted and very skilled but doesn't usually have a plan. He turns up and acts, or reacts. He might have to revise his ideas about how to keep on track and avoid being a victim rather than a victor, but it works for him in his uncertain world of double agents.
- **Sherlock Holmes** looks at each piece of evidence in detail and forensically builds up a picture of what happened and the characteristics of the criminal involved. He deduces others' motivations, needs, and problems from small details and then looks for further evidence to confirm or refute his ideas.

We can think of these as approaches to control, ways of ensuring that what these detectives want to happen does indeed happen—they gather good enough information to catch criminals and prove their guilt. People have different preferences for controlling their work and relationships and this is often the source of problems. If I encounter a James Bond and I am a Sherlock Holmes, we are unlikely to work well together. Finding ways to feel more comfortable using several of these approaches will not remove your preoccupation for control, but it might make it more tolerable for others.

Analytic Which detective?

Think about how you control your work. Does any detective seem pretty close to the approach you take? If you don't recognise your approach to control here, can you name a detective that you can identify with?

Identify a recent experience where you feel your preoccupation with control was unhelpful. Describe your approach to controlling what was happening using the language of the detectives.

On reflection, can you say which aspects of your approach were inappropriate and why?

Now imagine taking another approach, from a different detective.

What would you have to do to make this happen? Which of your routines and practices would you need to change?

6.4 Ways to work with my identity as an asset

Now we revisit those preoccupations with identity dynamics of recognition, regulation, and revelation to find ways to work with identity as an asset of professional practice.

6.4.1 Recognition: individual and organisational narratives

We talked earlier, in Chapter Four, about roles being located in the wings of our practice, like the props of a play. This idea builds on the performance imagery of "front-stage/back-stage" (Goffman, 1959): front-stage is the experience of being mind-fully present with the client, in a visible consulting and change relationship; backstage, the work that we do away from the client, through our own inner dialogues, conversations, and activities with colleagues. Stage performance is not the same as consulting, yet some of its analogies are helpful; being thrust into the limelight for instance, when a client suddenly focusses upon you, asking questions that you weren't expecting, or when you need to suddenly stand up and present something—on the hoof.

Shifting our work on our identities and presence between front-stage/backstage is a helpful strategy in working with issues related to recognition.

> Clive, who finds himself concentrating on his co-working relationship at the point when he is engaged in contracting with his client (see Chapter Two), knows that his attention is being taken up by having to manage his emotions rather than being present with the client. This is a front-stage dilemma but he needs to do some backroom thinking about who he is in this situation, in relation to both his co-worker and his client.

> Noele, whose past role as lecturer continues to guide and shape her mode of relating with her organisational clients (see Chapter Two) can also reorganise her front-stage/backstage work, to attempt a narrative that says—this is who I was, and this is who I am now. She might then also go on to say—this is who I might be, allowing herself a vision for her business development.

This activity is designed to help you reveal an aspect of your identity that you would like to experiment with. We can revitalise our understanding of "who I am" at any one time through the language we make use of in telling stories. Crafting a narrative about who I am is a temporary and provisional device—it doesn't fix me for all time.

Analytic Crafting a professional narrative.

> 1. Choose an artefact that represents an aspect of your professional identity as it is now. This can be your laptop, a plane ticket, a manual or report that you have written, a book you value, or something more personal, a photo, a gift.
> 2. Think about how to locate this artefact in a story about you that has a past and a present. What is its significance to you, how much do you identify with, or feel associated to the item. Can you continue with your story into the future? Will you still need or want the item, can you let it go?
> 3. If you are working in a peer group, or work discussion group, tell your story to a colleague or the group. How does the story come out now that you are speaking to this group? Have you changed it?
> 4. Ask for feedback as to how your colleagues have heard your story. Does it resonate with them? Does it surprise them? Is their interest captured? What sense can they make of your story: is it coherent or all over the place; is it so wrapped up that you don't leave any threads for exploration?
>
> If your story takes you into a different kind of future, think about how this sounds. Is this a story you can start to tell now—will it support experimentation with future possible identities?

Clive and Noele's stories together with the analytic activity illustrate preoccupations with "me", as an individual, and my identities at any one moment. But as consultants and change practitioners we work with colleagues, in organisations, in partnerships and alliances. My narrative in these contexts is only one thread of the many narratives that are going on simultaneously. My story might be starting where yours is about to end. Mine may be about to go off on a huge tangent—a relocation, a secondment, but I don't know it yet. Something significant about the environment in which my organisation is located may not have appeared on my radar; I haven't yet registered the implications of a government policy, or quite how the global economy, or the social protest movement might make itself felt in my particular neck of the woods.

Locating myself in time can help me notice who I am in relation to the shifting sands of organisational life. Here is a narrative structure that can work as a "projective device"—something where I can locate myself, but also gain some distance so as to allow for shifts and movements in my identity.

Box 6.4 Working with narrative structures	
Storyline	*Consultant repertoire*
What is the genre for my story? *For example: period drama, science fiction, fairy tale*	How am I viewing this scenario?
Who am I in the narrative? *For example: unknown narrator, protagonist, minor player*	Who am I as the consultant/change practitioner?
What is the plot? *What issues are the characters facing?*	How do I perceive the key issues in the client system? (or in the consultancy system)
How does the plot develop in relation to its characters and their dilemmas. Does the narrative style support the plot *For example: pace and timing, single/multiple storylines/voices*	How is change encountered, and how can I intervene? How can I access and work with multiple and complex threads of experience?
What kind of storyline am I in, and how does it influence outcomes? *For example: will all be revealed and sewn up, what threads continue?*	What kinds of outcomes are recognisable, valued and possible?

Kim is a partner in an SME, which offers IT solutions to improve business to business relations. The company is led by two partners, one with consulting expertise and knowledge of the sector, and one with technical knowledge. They have invested well in their technical design processes, but need to take the business forward in their business consulting offer. This is how Kim who holds the consulting/ sector expertise works with this narrative structure to bring to the surface ideas about where she can reshape her identity in relation to her partner role.

	Box 6.5 Kim's story	
Storyline	*Organisational repertoire*	*Data sourced from?*
What is the genre?	A film—a cold-war espionage thriller, in grainy black and white.	Experiences of client-facing activities: we have to make decisions over the offer of the company, and how we can create advantages for our clients in a way that purely technical companies can't.
Who am I in the narrative?	I'm a central character, though definitely not the lead. I also take various bit parts.	Rationale for company start up, and preliminary organisational structure. My expertise was invaluable in setting up the company, but it's hard to get myself to the table now. The technical has become dominant.
What is the plot?	A train is travelling across Europe, it gets held up at an international border, waiting to take on extra carriages and passengers. The train and its small number of passengers are vulnerable. Supplies are running low.	Business objective: to join up the two aspects of the business and have greater market presence in technical consulting challenges. Taking on new staff means that they have to be inducted, and contribute to business direction, but this takes time and resources.
How does the plot develop in relation to its characters and issues	I thought I was the driver, but now I seem to be acting as the guard. I have to be protective—this is an isolated and mountainous terrain, and spies could be anywhere. The passengers are getting frustrated waiting, and anxious that the train is delayed. They start to plan their own strategy for getting the train moving.	Where are we at with competitors? Mapping of stakeholders, where are they influencing? We don't pay as much attention to our clients/staff as we need to, their stories are missing—I probably don't want to give up my original ideas for the business to allow for new ideas to come in, it feels quite a threat.
What kind of storyline am I in, and how does it influence outcome	We have to overcome adversity. There is certainly no going back, we can only go forward. We run the risk that a passenger will attempt to drive the train, and then we would be in trouble.	Financial tracking—growth *vs* consolidation. The business will find its own direction, and I need to be in there with my colleagues, rather than trying to control what could happen.

Kim can see from the narrative that she lets her imagination construct, that she is getting caught up in safeguarding the business, rather that bringing herself as a leader to it. Her consulting abilities are stagnating, along with the business. She no longer feels that she has control, and is starting to put the damper on initiatives rather than accessing something more creative. This narrative structure as a projective device enables Kim to think about how she recognises herself in the company, and how she can start to make some shifts in revising her role.

Analytic Creating your own narrative.

Have a go at filling in the narrative structure (see Box 6.4 above) for your own consulting and change platform/organisation.

What does it reveal about "who you are" now?

What aspects of the narrative structure might you want to change? (the genre, who I am in the narrative, the plot, the characters, the storyline overall).

Shifts to any of these aspects of the narrative structure will allow for a playful reorganisation of identity. What opportunities do you see for revising who you are in this scenario?

Once you have some ideas, try telling this new story to your colleagues.

6.4.2 Regulation: managing inner and outer worlds

The saying "you are only as good as your last consultation, your last change assignment, your last educational workshop" can easily take up residence in our internal dialogues, as part of a low-grade and pervasive anxiety that Power and colleagues (2009) refer to as "reputational risk". Engagements that can allow for an off-day are rare.

Part of our practice relates to making judgements about how well we are working, in what kinds of situations, and with which kinds of issues. This relates to how well we can handle the uncertainties of organisational dilemmas, when most situations that we find ourselves working in have no easy success formulas. We then have choices about what kind of work we choose to take on, and the suitability of our skills, knowledge, and experience to work with the issues the client presents.

This "back of the envelope" equation in Figure 6.4 is one we have formulated to help think about, name, and explore reputational anxieties in our work, and to help us make choices about what work we do.

$$\frac{\textit{Primary Risk for Client of Enterprise}}{\textit{Credibility and authority of Consultant to work on Enterprise}} + \frac{\textit{Client's capacity for projection into Consultant}}{\textit{Consultant's capacity for projection into Client}} + \textit{Client, consultant existential Dread} = \textit{Reputational Risk}$$

© Karen Izod

Figure 6.4 Reputational risk.

Let's break this equation into its parts:

a) Primary risk of enterprise for client:

In this equation, the idea of the "enterprise" for the client relates to everything that is concerned with addressing this change, in this organisation. The "primary task" (Lawrence, G. W. 1985) of an organisation is what it has to do in order to be able to survive: this is evident in its rationales, stated purpose, and the ways in which its members understand and relate to the organisation. Rarely do organisations have single primary tasks, for example supermarkets might have a primary retail purpose, yet their car parks often have multiple purposes that include parking for customers, recycling facilities and occasional portakabin for libraries and health screening. Addressing which of these purposes are needed to ensure the survival of the organisation is not necessarily clear, relating as they do to use of land, customer good will, community cohesion. The risk associated with choosing between tasks and the possibility of selecting the wrong task is described as the "primary risk" (Hirschhorn, 1999).

> Here is how an HR business partner in the petro-chemical industry describes the primary risk he faces:
>
> "The decisions that are being made are about investment, which products in which markets. That's the company's primary risk. So because of that it's important that we choose which projects to take on with our business partners—so that we also stand a good chance of seeing a project through. Making this choice I would say, is the primary risk we face in our unit."

b) My credibility/authority to work on this enterprise:

This is where we face the issues we worked with in Chapter Three, presence, and how I can bring myself to work with credibility and authority on this enterprise. As for the client, enterprise here, relates to everything that I have to bring to address this desired change, in this organisation, including the recognition that actual change might look very different to desired change. Having credibility and authority in my field is one way of bringing containment to our work, so as to face the dilemmas our clients face in their enterprise.

> "I'm knowledgeable about the sector, but I'm not an expert in mergers. I don't yet know what the issues at stake are, and whether I will be able to work with them. It's a big unknown." *Health Sector specialist.*
>
> "I worry I'm a bit of a one-trick pony, too much of a generalist, and very little that is expert." *HR generalist, government agency.*

We are not necessarily going to know in advance, what risks we will encounter in taking on an assignment, but it is helpful to have a sense of which emotions I am going to need to regulate in myself as the assignment progresses. Spending time worrying about my competence and authority is going to reduce the attentiveness I can bring to the client.

Here is one way of thinking about what you might take on:

Analytic Credibility and authority to work.

> Name the primary risk that you believe your client faces in undertaking this enterprise. Or, make a hypothesis from the information that you have available to you at this point.
>
> Do you imagine that the work you will be required to do is:
>
> - In my comfort zone—that is, I have existing skills and experience to bring to the work
>
> - Would be a stretch—that is, I have ideas about how to do it, but don't have experience
>
> - Way outside—that is, I have no ideas and no experience about how to go about it.
>
> - Where are you going to draw a boundary in what you can take on?
>
> - Where do you see the limits of your credibility?
>
> - Where can you reasonably expect to extend your learning and experience in co-construction with your client?
>
> How can your identity and presence provide resources for you to bring to this work?

c) Capacity for projection into me, as consultant/change agent:

Here are some examples of where consultants feel that they are being projected into. You might want to refer back to Chapter Two for a reminder of the dynamics of projection.

> "Contracting with this client has been a nightmare, they want to sew everything up tightly, about what I can and can't do. I know that I'm a new supplier. They don't know me yet, but it's as if they are safeguarding themselves against all eventualities. All the risk for this project gets put onto me."
>
> "I feel that I should have all the data at my fingertips, so that I can advise them on what will work." *Self-employed change consultants.*

To some extent, it is inevitable that we help our clients manage the anxieties associated with change, and we have talked about this as a process of mutual containment, which enables both client and consultant to access their competencies (see Chapter Five). When we are overloaded with emotion, and feel "dumped upon" then it is more difficult to find our own competence. We may find ourselves in avoidance mode and reluctant to touch the work, much as we might behave with a sore tooth.

Trying to understand what belongs to me, and what belongs to the client, is something that we can attune ourselves to, by paying attention to which emotions we are easily in touch with in ourselves, and which can be easily mobilised by others. I can't prevent my clients from projecting their fears and desires into me, only to be aware of when this might be happening, and to recognise that it is an important piece of data. Asking myself "what does this feeling or experience represent in this encounter?" can be enough to shift myself out of paralysing emotions and dynamics, by trying to find meaning in them. In the above example of the contracting nightmare, it might be enough to raise the subject of risk and how we as client and consultant, can act as barometers of risk for each other, which can then allow the client to start to own, and to take back, their projections.

d) Capacity for projection into client:

As with the client projecting into me, then so there is a risk involved in projecting into the client. If the client is going to have to carry emotions for me, and for the work, then it's likely that the client won't want to work closely with me, and I will be compromising the efficacy of my practice.

> "The chief operating officers are all very knowledgeable, they know all the tricks of the trade, and they make a very powerful clique. I don't see how anything I could say will make a difference." *Internal consultant, global manufacturing company.*
>
> "The company director is never available when I ask to meet him, I know he's very busy, and probably doesn't want to bother with this. Perhaps I'll work with the HR director instead". *Niche consultant, contracting for a company wide intervention.*

In these examples, there is no reason to suspect that perceptions about the clients, in the minds of the consultants, are in any way inaccurate. The chief operating officers (COO) may make a powerful clique, the company director (CD) almost definitely will have a busy schedule. The issue is more about how we relate to these perceptions. Do we regard them as a truth, and not challenge them? Do we use them to make excuses for ourselves so as not to take a more courageous route with a client? I'm really too ambivalent about this assignment to present myself to the CD, so I will let myself be put off by his busy diary. In this scenario, it is easier to assume that the CD is busy, than it is to face my ambivalence about what I might need to talk with him about. Checking out our assumptions and fantasies about our clients, and wondering what they might mean, is one way to start to own our projections, and acknowledge what they indicate for our practice.

e) Client/consultant existential concerns:

Existential concerns are those concerns that we face about our survival in life. Am I earning enough money to pay my bills this month? What am I going to do if my course doesn't recruit enough participants this year? What will happen when the lease on my office runs out; where else can I locate my business? These are concerns that with a bit of thinking we can find names for, understand that these anxieties are inevitable, and that with sufficient resourcefulness we can apply ourselves to managing these stressful events. They often influence decisions as to what work we do, and push us into being instrumental, that is, letting our work meet our own survival needs. This is how we can sometimes get into inappropriate and opportunistic work that may not bear much relation to our credibility and skills to do it.

> "I need to do well with my 'happy sheets', if I dip down below a certain score, then they won't invite me back. With this level of uncertainty about the volume of work I can rely on then I'm permanently anxious." *Self-employed coach and trainer.*
>
> "My job is vulnerable: I might have to go with this next round of redundancies." *Public sector manager.*

At another level, existential concerns can also be unknown, the nameless dread that can wake us up early in the morning, which we cannot solve just by thinking about things, but that belongs to the human condition. Some of us will have more of a tendency to this kind of concern than others, but it is helpful to know what our tolerance for anxiety is. Taking on work that stretches this too far, will impact on my credibility, as will work that is boring and repetitive, which doesn't offer sufficient stimulation.

f) "Reputational risk" is a way of gauging my capacity to work with a client, based upon:

- My understanding of the risks the client is facing.
- My credibility to work with the issues the client presents in relation to these risks.
- My tendencies to project emotions into the client and their tendencies to project emotions into me.
- My tolerance for anxiety, based on my current circumstances, and the security of my platform for work.

114 RESOURCE-FUL CONSULTING

Analytic Analysing your reputational risk.

> Work through the reputational risk equation, identifying the risks that you are aware of, or might hypothesise at each point in relation to a particular consulting assignment.
>
> Using the dynamics of identity, think about how the resources they offer can support you in working with these risks:
>
> Recognition—am I recognisable in this case? What identities am I able to make use of with this client?
>
> Regulation—what emotions am I having to manage and what meaning might I be able to give to them in this context?
>
> Revelation—what changes in my identity might I need to consider? Am I giving myself sufficient role space to experiment with what might be needed?

6.4.3 Revelation

6.4.3a Being in touch, staying in touch

Being in touch with our emotions, as we are feeling them, is one of the most potent attributes that we can develop as a consultant, enabling us to work "front stage" with the dynamics of the moment. Which emotions will be triggered in us depends on the range of emotions that we have developed in infancy, and how our natural defences come into play to protect us from being overwhelmed by pleasure, anxiety, distress, and threat.

When work is going well, and I feel alive, curious, passionate about what I am doing, this is a delight, something to enjoy. Even in these moments, I may be hit by sudden feelings of remorse if I have spoken out thoughtlessly, or my chest can be tight with knowing I need to take a risk but fearing the way it will go.

Often there is a delay between our experience and being in touch with the feelings it generates: I might find myself going along with a client's enthusiasm in a meeting only to find myself instantly deflated when I step out of the door. I might agree to take on a piece of work, only later to be filled with dread about what it involves. I can't feel the concern in the moment, only once I have some space, or have let go of an inner control, sufficient to let my feelings come to the fore.

Owning up to ourselves about the kinds of emotions that are evoked in us by our work can be hard, particularly if it goes against some of the beliefs we hold dear. We may feel very irritated by a client that we have worked hard to have included, and then find ourselves wanting to exclude them. We may feel vulnerable when someone is forcing their view upon us and find that we withdraw. We may be embarrassed by an over-appreciative client and want to shake them off.

Emotions, when we can access them, serve as a litmus paper as to what might be going on in our clients, and in ourselves, that cannot necessarily be talked about, or thought about. Knowing my emotional range is helpful when it comes to identifying how the emotions I am feeling are being generated, and in turn, how my emotions are influencing my mode of relating to others.

Virginia Woolf (1931) in her essay collection "Killing the angel in the house" noticed how she came up against a demanding inner voice that required her to be kind to the authors whose work she reviewed. She embodied this inner voice as an ever-present angel: "She was intensely sympathetic. She was immensely charming. She was utterly unselfish" (Woolf, 1931, p. 3). She came to see that these personifications of her emotional responses to her work were not only unhelpful, but denied her access to a whole range of emotions, palatable or not, but which she nevertheless needed to draw upon to work authentically. "It was she who bothered me and wasted my time and so tormented me that at last I killed her". (Woolf, 1931, p. 3)

Personifying these inner voices is a way to notice which emotions are easily mobilised in us, and then to start to think about what else we might need to let into our emotional range. Here is some imagery we have played with.

- A parrot, always on my shoulder, always interrupting my serious side.
- A peacekeeper, trying to prevent outright warfare.
- A swashbuckling pirate, always looking for adventure, never keen to stay with anything for long.
- A traffic warden, quick to put a clamp on ideas before I give them any room.
- An after dinner speaker, has to be interesting, come up with witty observations—(but I don't charge that much).
- A Pollyanna, endlessly being optimistic, helpful and kind.

116 RESOURCE-FUL CONSULTING

Analytic Working with your angels and devils.

> Try this activity in conversation with a colleague. Identity the emotions that you are in touch with as you attempt to work with a client or on a task (this task maybe).
>
> Identify how these emotions turn into ways of relating (your inner voice telling you how to behave)
>
> Create a persona for your inner voice.
>
> Then:
>
> Position yourself on a scale of 1–5, to indicate the extent to which this inner voice is present now.
>
> Position yourself on a scale of 1–5, to indicate the extent to which you would like this inner voice to be present.
>
> In a group, this is best done with taking up a position in a line of chairs. Have your colleagues sit on a chair to indicate the extent to which your persona also exists in their repertoire.

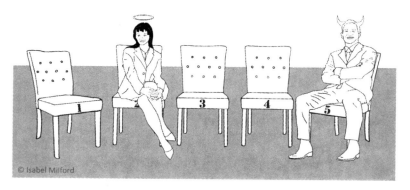

Figure 6.5 Angels and devils.

Virginia Woolf needed to get rid of her "Angel in the House" to allow for something more edgy, and outspoken to come in. She was able to acknowledge that for her to be creative she also had to access potentially destructive emotions and give them a place in her house in the persona of the Devil (Parker, 2007). You may have found in the positioning exercise above that your personas had both positive and negative attributes; the restless adventuring of the pirate, also has a go-getting quality, ruthless as it may be. You may sense that you need to allow in the polar opposite, a peacekeeper may need to let in the side of her that can be energised by conflict.

Try the activity again, identifying the devil (and its equivalent) that you need to bring into your work, and the extent to which it is present, or might need to be present. Here are some examples of devils:

- Someone more humorous, more outspoken—a market trader.
- A mischievous, leprechaun side to me, I rarely let it out!
- Letting myself out without my makeup (metaphorically) be less than perfect, even allowing myself to not know, not have the answers.

When we attempt shifts of this kind, then we can come up against our own resistance to change. The Bartholomew & Horowitz grid (p. 86 this volume) offers a way of looking at how we respond to change, in particular acknowledging tendencies to have a positive/negative view of self, and a positive/negative view of others. When we have a secure attachment pattern, it is easier to respond to our curiosity, than when we are naturally cautious, or fearful of what change may bring.

6.5 Conclusion

As we have worked through our proposition—that how we bring ourselves to consulting work and use our presence is shaped by the dynamics of identity and authority—we have noticed that:

- Self confidence is a preoccupation evoked by dynamics of feeling over-whelmed.
- Competition is a preoccupation evoked by dynamics of feeling inferior.
- Control is a preoccupation evoked by dynamics of loss/annihilation.

These are feelings that resonate in our inner worlds, evoked either by our present encounters with our clients and the world of work, or belong in past traces of memory and experience. As such, ideas about regulation, how we can manage the boundary between inner and outer worlds, becomes a key resource in how we practice. Allowing for a boundary is something that we actively promote, in the use of a symbolic potential space, where possibilities for change and transformation reside.

Here we can experiment with who we are and who we are not to bring our multiple, yet recognisable selves to our work, revealing our identities by coming out from behind static roles, and crafting a presence that is fit for our purpose.

Notes

1. Karpman drama triangle. See http://karpmandramatriangle.com/pdf/DramaTriangle.pdf and http://coachingsupervisionacademy.com/thought-leadership/the-karpman-drama-triangle/
2. From *Action Science: Concepts, Methods, and Skills for Research and Intervention*, by Chris Argyris, Robert Putnam, and Diana McLain Smith Jossey-Bass 1985. See http://actiondesign.com/assets/pdf/AScha3.pdf and http://actiondesign.com/resources/research/action-science

CHAPTER SEVEN

Future developments

Susan Rosina Whittle

This is a book about consulting to organisations—consulting to the tasks and processes of change, where the self is an essential tool of consulting practice. In working through the chapters, we have invited you to get to know yourself better by exploring your:

- Identities—who I am I, and who I am not at any one time
- Presence—how I bring myself to my work and how people encounter me
- Preoccupations—what I am usually in touch with, through my thoughts and feelings, and what I habitually ignore or avoid.

This chapter invites you to bring together what you have found out about yourself in working through this book. It helps you construct a development agenda against nine essential competencies for using yourself as an instrument. We end by encouraging you to watch out for shame, as a dynamic that can sink your developmental intentions, and to work with the narratives you use to help you tell different and developmental stories about yourself and your consulting practice.

Preparing for the future

In *Mind-ful Consulting* (Whittle & Izod, 2009), a collection of edited stories from consultants working within the Tavistock tradition, we emphasised a number of practice challenges:

- To be present in the moment, disentangling our attention from the past and the future
- To be alert to the complacency of routine and undermining of complexity
- To be aware of the limitations of restrictive mind-sets and the constraints for creativity they pose.

Since we published *Mind-ful Consulting* in 2009:

- Barack Obama has been elected President of the Unites States, not once but twice
- We have the Euro Crisis, with depositors in Cypress waking up to find their bank accounts raided by the State
- The London Olympics and the fantastic Para Olympics have been and gone
- The Arab Spring is still rumbling (forward)
- Hugo Chávez, the President of Venezuela since 1999, has died
- A pope has resigned, the first in 600 years
- The UK was embroiled in a triple-dip recession
- NASA had flown its last space shuttle mission
- China is bankrolling Africa and America
- The Rolling Stones have completed a sell out fiftieth anniversary tour.

Clearly, what has happened in the past offers few, if any, clues about the future. As practitioners in consulting and change, we need to notice when we are stuck—in routines, practices, identities. We need to notice how our clients and colleagues encounter us—and work with it. We cannot imagine the future. But we can prepare to be surprised by and able to engage with the present, rather than reliving the past.

As educators and experts in professional development in this community of practice, it is our responsibility to be ahead of the curve. We need to notice what's on the horizon and equip consultants with the resources they need to work in the contexts they may encounter. The nature of these contexts is impossible to predict—other than that they will involve novelty, paradoxes, risks, and be incredibly fast paced. More and more consultants will work in "hyper-turbulent environments" (McCann & Selsky, 1984), where unforeseen events, perverse consequences, and vortical movements can create a fear of not knowing (Owers, 2009).

In these conditions, we can easily be overwhelmed and feel lost and cling to those ideas and practices that offer certainty, even if they are obsolete and ineffective; "better the Devil you know?" When something no longer works, the temptation is to look for another set of prescriptions to replace those that are obsolete. The consulting world is not short of ready-made solutions (Gill & Whittle, 1993). For example, resilience is a fashionable idea as we write this book.

Box 7.1 The fashion for resilience

In April 2013, resilience was the topic of the book reviews section in the UK's *Management Today* magazine. One of the books has a boomerang on the cover. It describes resilience as "bouncing back" from the difficulties of life to emerge "relatively unscathed and ready to face positively the next challenge" (Webb, 2013, p. x). Bouncing back is not about learning and development. Resilience is about keeping going and not being deflected by whatever comes your way. This highlights the difference between resilience and the resource-ful approach we take.

Resource-ful consulting requires the management and renewal of assets, and being ready to leave behind those which limit and constrain.

In this chapter, we outline a set of competencies we use to help practitioners hone their use of "self-as-instrument" (Cheung-Judge, 2001) and offer an opportunity for you to bring together your insights and evaluations in a development agenda.

7.1 A professional development agenda for practitioners of consulting and change

How clients and colleagues encounter me has significant implications for my consulting practice. I need to think about how others experience me and how my presence helps or hinders my crafting a context that is both appropriately reassuring and sufficiently challenging to support their work, development, and change. This requires me to work with my presence as intervention, presence that is designed to help something happen (Chapter Three, this book).

To consult effectively, I need to own my presence. I need to think about my presence as the active presentation of myself in relation to my clients and colleagues and the task(s) we are working on. Preoccupations with identity and authority can undermine presence as intervention. This makes identity and authority focal points for professional development. In *Resourceful Consulting*, we have experimented with creating a potential space to help you: step-back from your existing practices; question your routines; and renew how you work with identity, authority, and presence. Our working model is shown in Figure 7.1.

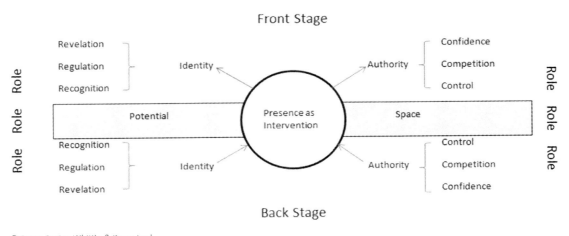

Figure 7.1 Presence as intervention.

"Working with the dynamics of identity, presence, and role" is one category of the competency model we use in assessment for the Practitioner Certificate in Consulting and Change. The full model requires candidates to demonstrate their use of self-as-instrument in their work by incorporating all nine categories of the model into their practice. The categories are shown in Table 7.1.

Table 7.1 Nine categories to demonstrate use of "self-as-instrument" in practice.

1	Working with the dynamics of identity, presence, and role
2	Paying attention to consulting cycle dynamics at entry and contracting and through to exit by:
3	Using data and analysis
4	Using concepts and theories for sense-making, hypothesis formulation, and experimentation
5	Making use of "here-and now" and "then and there" experiences
6	Crafting and creating intervention designs
7	Understanding risk, accountability, and the politics of change
8	Working with learning and regression, including the nature of perpetual preoccupations in self and client systems
9	Working with evaluations, exits, and emotions.

Analytic Development analysis.

Look at each of the categories below demonstrating use of "self-as-instrument". In which categories do you have strengths as a consultant/change professional? Make a note in the chart below.

Also note categories that are missing from your practice or where you find yourself demonstrating less competence than you would like and have some concerns.

(You might want to look back at your professional development agendas from Chapter Three).

1   Working with the dynamics of identity, presence, and role

2   Paying attention to consulting cycle dynamics at entry and contracting and through to exit by:

3   Using data and analysis

4   Using of concepts and theories for sense-making, hypothesis formulation, and experimentation

5   Making use of "here-and-now" and "then and there" experiences

6   Crafting and creating intervention designs

7   Understanding risk, accountability, and the politics of change

8   Working with learning and regression, including the nature of perpetual preoccupations in self and client systems

9   Working with evaluations, exits, and emotions.

124 RESOURCE-FUL CONSULTING

Analytic Plotting development needs.

> Now transfer your strengths and concerns onto the radar chart shown in Figure 7.2.
>
> Choose a score for each category and mark it on the chart; the greater your assessment of your competence, the higher the score (towards the outer rim of the chart).
>
> What does this reveal to you about where you need to focus your professional development activities?

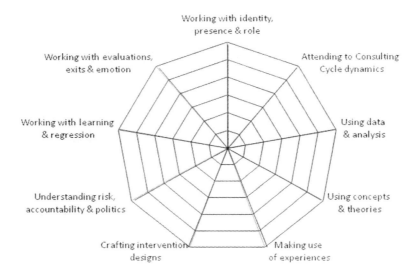

Figure 7.2 What's on my radar?

The priority given to your development needs changes as clients, sectors, and their issues change. Can you translate your development needs from the radar chart into specific agendas for the types of work you see on the horizon? Some examples are shown in Box 7.2.

Box 7.2 Development in context

"I am concerned that I'll bring a limited, eurocentric approach to international work. I worry that I don't have the breadth of experience and the cultural know-how. I need to start thinking of my identity and working on my presence more globally."

"How do I redesign my professional development programmes to continue to attract internal clients now they have access to external suppliers? I need to think about how the interventions I design can appeal to our new situation and rethink my roles—maybe to broker."

"We know very little about evaluation as consulting practice and have not really thought about exits. Given what's happening in our particular part of the public sector at the moment, this is something we need to address and make part of our everyday thinking."

Analytic My development in context.

Now try making some statements of the sort in Box 7.2 that relate your development to your own context.

7.3 What to watch out for

Preoccupations depend on routines and practices to maintain my assumptions and beliefs and my sense of my world. These routines detect threats and risks to the presence and identities I have honed over the years and to which I am attached. Any undermining of my sense of myself is likely to evoke a strong reaction—shame. Shame is "a sense of inadequacy of the self, of not being up to the task or of being defective". (Hunt, 2000).

Others can make me feel guilty or embarrassed but only I can make myself feel shame. This is because shame resides in the mismatch between the self I experience and my ideal self (see page 36 in this book).

I feel shame when I look at myself and don't like what I see. If my idealised self always makes a good profit, or delivers projects on time and budget, or retains a difficult client by being creative, when these things don't happen I can feel shame. I don't measure up.

Shame anxiety is the feeling of inadequacy I get when I anticipate I might fail and I will feel bad. My inner voice is recounting a tale of loss. I can contain shame anxiety and protect my idealised self by not trying. Watch out for shame anxiety! It can stop your development before you start.

Shame anxiety is not something that can be worked with alone. Group analysis offers a particularly helpful approach to identifying and working with shame for change practitioners.[1]

7.3 Using narratives

The tales we tell ourselves shape our development and the risks we take. Each of the statements in Box 7.2 contains a story line, a very short tale about a problem and ideas about how to resolve that problem. The plots or narrative structures are hopeful in their desire to overcome some adversity. It's said that authors only have a limited number of plots to choose from. Polti (1916) put this number at thirty-six. Some are shown in Box 7.3.

Box 7.3 Narrative plots		
• Deliverance • Vengeance of a crime • Falling prey to misfortune • Revolt • Daring enterprise	• Rivalry of kinsmen • Rivalry of superior and inferior • Madness • Self-sacrificing for an ideal	• Crimes of love • Discovery of the dishonour of a loved one • Ambition • Mistaken jealousy • Recovery of a lost one

How might we describe the plots in box 7.2? Are they plots about ambition, about deliverance, or daring enterprise; maybe a combination? Like everyone else, writers tend to have their favourite plots and become known for specific genre: maybe love stories, political dramas, or disaster movies. There are further choices to be made within a genre. A love story can start happily and end happily, or it can end unhappily. That a story can be told in different ways can be a revelation to many people. In working with professionals in consulting and change, we have found that being aware of just three narrative forms is enough to help them change the plot in their practice. These are the heroic tale, the tragedy and the comedy.

FUTURE DEVELOPMENTS 127

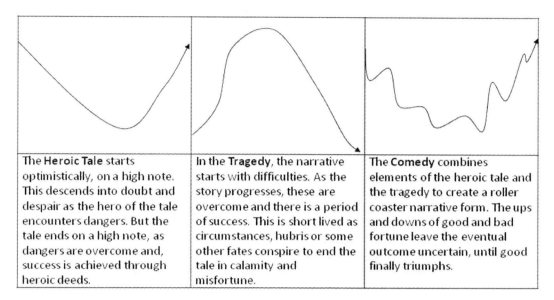

Figure 7.3 Three narrative forms.

Business magazines, academic journals, and case studies are full of heroic tales but there are few comedies and even fewer tragedies amongst the narratives. When talking about our own work, we tend to leave out tragedy narratives; it's not good for business. But if we are seeking to improve our practice we need to acknowledge and articulate our tales of when things go wrong, at least to our selves.

By stepping outside the narrative structure as a given and choosing which form to use, we are able to tell different stories to ourselves about ourselves. This developmental step is speeded up and taken much further if we can change the genre of our story (say from TV soap, to fairy tale, to horror move) as well as the narrative form.

> Emily worked hard to maintain a presence of victim. Her narrative was about being ignored for promotion, of not being able to speak to the right people, can't do this or that because … She was in tragedy mode and on a long trail to oblivion. Inviting her to retell a work experience using a comedy narrative, and transposing the story to the wild west, enabled Emily to cast herself differently, see some humour in her own tale, and explore alternative ways to end the story and think about her development.

The story I tell can help me to contain my anxieties (by being realistic rather than heroic) and to maintain a potential space for my development (by helping me to move between genres and plots).

Analytic Which narrative?

> Which one of the three narrative forms (heroic tale, tragedy, or comedy) do you tend you use most, with colleagues, with clients, in documents and presentations, in evaluations? (Ask your colleagues and clients if you are not sure.)
>
> Try talking to a colleague about a recent assignment you have both worked on as a comedy … What did you discover in the retelling?
>
> Now, can you talk about the same assignment using a different genre, maybe a romance, a detective story, a science fiction or murder mystery?
>
> Ask your colleagues what they notice about you when you are trying out different narrative forms.

Ending

Rather than offer prescriptions, we have invited you into a "playful" space to co-construct the value of *Resource-ful Consulting* by identifying situations where you are getting stuck and have difficulty making sense of what might be going on.

We have tried to do this in a book and recognise the limitations of this medium. Nevertheless, in *Resource-ful Consulting* we think we offer more than a taste of the ways in which we work to support change in change practitioners. The narratives that we have offered, and the approaches that we have taken, are real. They take place in real encounters between us as consultants in professional development and practitioners and their clients. It is a book of real life.

Our aim has been to help dispel temptations to "hide behind role" and the desire to control, compete, or withdraw in moments of anxiety, with a more functional and emotionally authentic engagement between consultant and client.

Good luck in developing your resources and working with your presence and identity. Let us know how you get on.

Note

1. See www.groupanalysis.org/ and www.groupanalyticpractice.ie

APPENDIX

P3C programme design

We designed The Tavistock Institute Practitioner Certificate in Consulting and Change (P3C) as a residential programme of five short modules over nine months. As founders, we directed four cohorts of the programme between 2009–2013.

The modules combined established Tavistock know-how with contemporary innovations in theory and practice across five core themes: organising, changing, doing, knowing, and evaluating. Each module focussed on dynamics of the consulting cycle, explored through classic Tavistock texts and our recent thinking about practice. Modules themes are shown in Box App 1.

Box App 1 P3C module themes
Module 1: Entry and contracting and the dynamics of power and containment
Module 2: Data and analysis and the dynamics of credibility and competition
Module 3: Interventions and the dynamics of risk and accountability
Module 4: Learning and regression and the dynamics of sustainability
Module 5: Evaluation and exit and the dynamics of endings and loss.

In designing the P3C programme, we drew on well-known Tavistock expertise in individual learning, group development, and organisation change. Our aim was to offer a professional development programme for consultants, leaders, and professional managers looking to enhance their consulting and change management practices by working with their presence and identity. With an experiential and collaborative design, participants numbers were limited to ten per cohort, working with the same two directors throughout.

Programme participants worked with concepts and theories from the three Tavistock Anthologies, *The Socio Psychological Perspective, The Socio Technical Perspective,* and *The Socio Ecological Perspective*[1] and a range of contemporary narratives to:

1. Analyse behaviours in organisational systems under going change and
2. Design developmental interventions for individuals, groups, and organisations.

This experiential programme was designed to help participants use themselves as instruments to achieve change in their client systems. Through collaboration with each other and with programme directors, they were encouraged to make use of the opportunities provided in the programme to develop a mind-ful approach to their consulting practice. They worked on clarifying the choices, constraints, habits, and compulsions shaping their professional work.

Who was P3C programme designed for?

We invited applications from people working in consulting and change:

- Who noticed that:
  - They found themselves surprised by clients, contracts, or themselves.
  - Their attention frequently shifted between attending to the vital and the virtual.
  - They were struggling to find relevant theoretical frameworks to help them understand their experiences and inform their interventions.
  - Their authority is sometimes compromised.
  - They needed to be challenged and to renew their professional identity.
- Who were interested in using here-and-now experiences to:
  - Experiment with group learning and development, by integrating organisational and psychodynamic theories with practical change and consulting perspectives.
  - Explore role taking and contracting to enable you to contribute to programme content. You will design programme interventions to learn about real issues in working with emerging challenges in consultancy and change.
  - Develop a mind-ful approach by using the self as instrument and maintaining a grounded presence whilst immersing yourself in complex, fast-paced organisational dynamics.

As experienced consultants and organisation change practitioners, educators, and academics, we pledged to provide the structures and frameworks for P3C participants to explore ideas and understand their own repertoires. We announced that we would craft the learning environment and content together and work on current practice issues and professional development needs.

We described P3C as offering a potential space (Winnicott, 1953), in which careful listening (to hear feelings), attention to timing, and playfulness were some of the skills we would be working on. Specifically we contracted that we would help each participant to:

- Understand your own repertoire.
- Build on what you know already.
- Reach beyond what you know and are comfortable with.
- Develop your authority, presence, your use of data, and your skills in contracting, containment, and intervention.
- Internalise and apply your development in your work.

Who did the P3C programme attract?

Between 2009 and 2013, the P3C programme attracted four full cohorts of ten people. These forty participants came from diverse professional domains. Each one already possessed substantial consulting experience, along with professional or academic qualification, and was looking to improve their practical skills, theoretical confidence, and authoritative presence. The types of consulting practice, nationalities, expertise and sectors represented are shown in Box App 2.

Box App 2 P3C participant characteristics			
Types of practice	*Nationalities*	*Examples of expertise*	*Sectors*
Internal consultants	American	Coaching	Communications
External consultants	Argentinean	Communications	Construction
Change leaders	Canadian	Culture change	Consulting
HR specialists	Dutch	Financial management	Defence
OD specialists	English	Fundraising & events	Education
Strategy specialists	Finish	Group facilitation	Electronics
Leadership specialists	French	Information technologies	Government
Consultants in global firms	German	Leadership development	Health
Owners of small consulting firms	Irish	Marketing and branding	Housing
Sole traders	Italian	Mediation	Insurance
Consultants in transition from:	Japanese	Mergers and partnerships	IT
• internal role to external role	Norwegian	Negotiation	Manufacturing
	Russian	Organisation change	Not-For-Profit
• global firm to own business	Scottish	Outdoor training	Petroleum
	South African	Paediatrics	Pharmaceuticals
• media to insurance sectors	Swiss	Performance improvement	Prison services
		Process design	Probation
• clinical work to corporate work		Project management	Retail
		Psychometrics	Social care
		Quality management	Television
		Redundancy	Training
		Restructuring	University
		Start-up	
		Strategic planning	
		Team development	

What did we do?

Consecutive modules built on emergent learning, stubborn issues, and practice needs identified in previous residential sessions to address the following questions:

o Where am I—what organisation am I working in? How do I describe it? What makes sense?
o How am I doing the work? What approaches, methods, tools, and techniques am I using, how did I choose them and why?
o How well am I doing and how do I know?
o Can I improve my practice? What do I need to work on?

These were explored through experiential activities, peer review, consultations to practice and relevant theoretical inputs. Throughout the programme, participants were invited to step into both consultant and client roles and draw on their professional and personal experiences to contribute to each other's development. Further opportunities were provided for individuals to consult to group task and process.

As might be expected from a Tavistock programme, the dynamics between participants and between participants and staff were constantly available for analysis, as a live example of the typical challenges encountered in working with individual, group, organisational, and technological change. The design provided opportunities for giving and receiving feedback on professional persona, technical skills, and process expertise.

Typical learning objectives included: learning to manage and contain myself in role; learning how to contain others; using my past and "here and now" experiences to inform my analyses; applying psychodynamic intelligence to guide my actions and interventions and understanding the dynamics relating to co-construction of interventions between client and consultant.

Exploring the dynamics between participants and between participants and staff, meant that we needed to attend to multiple layers of experience to notice what a practitioner might need to address in their development, and how we could work with them to bring about change. These are outlined in Box App. 3 below.

Box App 3 Layers of experience

What we encounter in our experience of consulting to the professional development of change practitioners (here and now)

What change practitioners are encountering as they work together and with us on their professional development (here and now)

What change practitioners and we bring with us from our experiences in attempting to bring about change in organisations (there and then)

What change practitioners and we bring with us of our everyday experiences of organisational life (there and then).

We worked with participant's typical learning objectives through these layers of "here and now", "there and then" in what we call the experiential learning LABS. These "double task" (Bridger, 1990) activities enable us to work on our thoughts and feelings about how we are working, as we are attempting to work on a consulting task. Participating as consultants in the LABS gives us clues about the kinds of "embodied" experiences change practitioners are meeting in their work, and opportunities to try out new ways of thinking and behaving in the moment. This kind of LAB experience has to be entered into for oneself. I can only find ways to hone my "self-as-instrument" by learning from my experience. I can't learn vicariously from yours.

Note

1. http://moderntimesworkplace.com/archives/archives.html

WEB RESOURCES

www.actiondesign.com/assets/pdf/AScha3.pdf last accessed 21 November 2013.
www.actiondesign.com/resources/research/action-science last accessed 21 November 2013.
www.bbc.co.uk/programmes/b007qgcl/clips last accessed 21 November 2013.
www.businessballs.com/johariwindowmodel.htm last accessed 21 November 2013.
www.cfar.com/cf/index.cfm?fuseaction=Publications.viewMostRecentPublications last accessed 30 March 2013.
www.changingminds.org/disciplines/storytelling/plots/polti_situations/polti_situations.htm last accessed 8 October 2013.
www.changingminds.org/explanations/identity/jung_archetypes.htm last accessed 21 November 2013.
www.channel4.com/news/tarantino-uncut-when-quentin-met-krishnan-transcript last accessed 21 November 2013.
www.coachingsupervisionacademy.com/thought-leadership/the-karpman-drama-triangle/ last accessed 21 November 2013.
www.contemporarypsychotherapy.org/vol-2-no-2/negative-capability/ last accessed 16 May 2013.
www.dictionary.cambridge.org/dictionary/british/inference last accessed 13 May 2013.
www.iep.utm.edu/lacweb/#SH4a last accessed 23 May 2013.
www.irishexaminer.com/opinion/columnists/terry-prone/opinion-questions-to-be-asked-about-celebs-right-not-to-reply-219456.html 01/14/2013 last accessed 28 January 2013.
www.groupanalysis.org last accessed 21 November 2013.
www.groupanalyticpractice.ie last accessed 21 November 2013.
www.guardian.co.uk/film/2013/jan/11/tarantino-krishnan-guru-murthy?INTCMP=SRCH last accessed 29 January 2013.
www.karpmandramatriangle.com/pdf/DramaTriangle.pdf last accessed 21 November 2013.
www.moderntimesworkplace.com/archives/archives.html last accessed 8 October 2013.

www.news.bbc.co.uk/1/hi/7782422.stm last accessed 21 November 2013.
www.postsecret.com last accessed 21 November 2013.
www.sloanreview.mit.edu/article/the-effective-organization-forces-and-forms/ last accessed 24 May 2013.
www.systems-thinking.org/loi/loi.htm last accessed 8 October 2013.
http://www.ted.com/talks/itay_talgam_lead_like_the_great_conductors.html
www.worklab.com/wp-content/uploads/2009/12/Role-Consultation-Article2.pdf

REFERENCES

Alder, A. (2010). *Pattern Making, Pattern Breaking: Using Past Experience and New Behaviour in Training Education and Change Management.* Farnham: Gower.
Anderson, H. (2011). Never heard of FOMO? *The Observer Newspaper.* 11 April 2011.
Argyris, C. (1992). *Overcoming Organizational Defences.* New Jersey: Prentice Hall.
Argyris, C., & Schon, D. (1974). *Theory in Practice. Increasing Professional Effectiveness*, San Francisco: Jossey-Bass.
Bartholomew, K., & Horowitz, L. (1991). Attachment styles among young adults, a test of a four-category model. *Journal of Personality and Social Psychology, 61,* 2: 226–244.
Bateson, G. (1973). *Steps to an Ecology of the Mind.* London: Paladin.
Beech, N., Burns, H., de Caestecker, L., MacIntosh, R., & MacLean, D. (2004). Paradox as invitation to act in problematic change situations. *Human Relations, 57,* 10: 1313–1332.
Benjamin, J. (1998). *The Shadow of the Other: Intersubjectivity and Gender in Psychoanalysis.* New York: Routledge.
Benne, K., & Chin, R. (1985). Strategies of change. In: W. Bennis, K. Benne, & R. Chin, (Eds.), *The Planning of Change* (pp. 32–59). New York: International Thompson Publishing.
Berg, D. N. (2002). Bringing one's self to work: A Jew reflects. *The Journal Of Applied Behavioral Science, 38,* 4: 397–415.
Bion, W. R. (1999). Seminar held in Paris, 10 July 1978. Transcribed by Francesca Bion, September.
Block, P. (2000). *Flawless Consulting.* San Francisco: Jossey-Bass/Pfeiffer.
Bowlby, J. (1969). *Attachment and Loss Volume 1: Attachment.* London: Hogarth.
Bowlby, J. (1980). *Attachment and Loss, Volume 3: Loss, Sadness and Depression.* New York: Basic Books.
Bowlby, J. (1988). *A Secure Base, Clinical Applications of Attachment Theory.* London: Routledge.

Bridger, H. (1990). Courses and working conferences as transitional learning institutions. In: E. Trist & H. Murray (Eds.), *The Social Engagement of Social Science: A Tavistock Anthology. Volume 1: The Socio-Psychological Perspective*, (pp. 221–245). PA: University of Pennsylvania Press.

Cheung-Judge, Mee-Yan. (2001). The self as an instrument, a cornerstone for the future of OD. *OD Practitioner*, 33, 3: 11–16.

Clarke, S. (2009). Psycho-social research: relating self, identity and otherness. In: S. Clarke, H. Hahn & P. Hoggett (Eds.), *Object Relations and Social Relations* (pp. 113–136). London: Karnac.

Clarke, S., Hahn, H., Hoggett, P. (2009). *Object Relations and Social Relations*. London: Karnac.

Cohen, W. M., & Levinthal, D. A. (1990). Absorptive capacity: A new perspective on learning and innovation. *Administrative Science Quarterly*, 35, 1: 128–152.

Crombie, A. (1993). Active maladaptive strategies. In: E. Trist & H. Murray (Eds.), *The Social Engagement of Social Science, Volume 3: The Socio-Ecological Perspective*. London: Tavistock Publications.

Cummings, T. G., & Worley, C. G. (2008). *Organization Development & Change* (9th edition). Mason, OH: South-Western.

Diamond, M. A. (2008). Telling them what they know. Organizational change, defensive resistance, and the unthought known. *Journal of Applied Behavioral Science*, 44, 3: 348–364.

Dick, P. K. (1956). *Minority Report*. In: *Fantastic Universe*. US: King-Star Publications.

Emery F. E., & Trist, E. L. (1965). The causal texture of organizational environments. *Human Relations* 18: 21–23.

Fonagy, P., Gergely, G., Jurist, E. L. & Target, M. (2004). *Affect Regulation, Mentalization, and the Development of the Self*. London: Karnac.

French, R. (2000). Negative capability, dispersal and the containment of emotion. ISPSO Symposium, London.

Gergen, K. J., & Kaye, J. (1992). Beyond narrative in the negotiation of therapeutic meaning. In: S. McNamee & K. J. Gergen (Eds.), *Therapy as Social Construction* (pp. 166–186). London: Sage.

Giddens, A. (1991). *Modernity and Self-Identity: Self and Society in the Late Modern Age*. Cambridge: Polity Press.

Gill, J., & Whittle, S. (1993). Management by Panacea: Accounting for transience. *Journal of Management Studies*, 30: 281–295.

Goffman, E. (1959). *The Presentation of Self in Everyday Life*. New York: Doubleday Anchor Books.

Grueneisen, V., & Izod, K. (2009). Power dynamics of expertise and containment. In: S. Whittle & K. Izod (Eds.), *Mind-ful Consulting*. (pp. 57–74). London: Karnac.

Harris, A. (2010). *Romantic Moderns; English Writers, Artists and the Imagination from Virginia Woolf to John Piper*. London: Thames Hudson Ltd.

Hatch, M. J., & Schultz, M. (2002). The Dynamics of Organizational Identity, *Human Relations*, 55, 8: 989–1018.

Heron, J. (2001). *Helping the Client: A Practical Creative Guide* (5th edition). London: Sage.

Hirschhorn, L. (1988). *The Workplace Within: Psychodynamics of Organizational Life*. Cambridge, MA: MIT Press.

Hirschhorn, L. (1998). *Reworking Authority: Leading and Following in the Post-modern Organization*. Cambridge, MA: MIT Press.

Hirschhorn, L. (1999). The Primary Risk, *Human Relations*, 52, 1: 5–23.

Hoggett, P. (2006). Conflict, ambivalence and the contested purpose of public organisations. *Human Relations*, 59, 2: 175–194.

Horney, K. (1950). *Neurosis and Human Growth*. New York: Norton.

Hunt, J. (2000). Organizational leadership and shame. Paper to 17th Annual Meeting of the International Society for the Psychoanalytic Study of Organizations: London.

Ibarra, H. & Petriglieri, J. L. (2007). *Impossible Selves: Image strategies and identity threat in professional women's career transitions*. INSEAD Working Paper series 2007/69/OB.

Izod, K. (2009). How does a turn towards relational thinking influence consulting in organisations and groups? In: S. Clarke, H. Hahn & P. Hoggett (Eds.), *Object Relations and Social Relations* (pp. 163–184). London: Karnac.

Izod, K. (2013). Too close for comfort: Attending to boundaries in associate relationships. In: S. R. Whittle & R. C. Stevens (Eds.), *Changing Organizations from Within: Roles, Risks, and Consultancy Relationships* (pp. 145–163). Farnham: Gower.

Jacobs, M. L. (2005). *The Presenting Past: The Core of Psychodynamic Counselling and Therapy*. Maidenhead, UK: Open University Press.

Jung, C. G. (1951). *Aion: Researches into the Phenomenology of the Self*. London: Routledge & Kegan Paul.

Kahn, W. (1992). To be fully there: psychological presence at work. *Human Relations*, 45: 321–349.

Katz, D., & Kahn R. L. (1978). *The Social Psychology of Organizations*. New York: Wiley.

Kets de Vries, M. F. R., & Miller, D. (1984). *The Neurotic Organization*. San Francisco, CA: Jossey-Bass.

Kirkpatrick, D. (1994). *Evaluating Training Programs*. San Fransisco, CA: Berrett-Koehler.

Kohut, H. (1984). *How Does Analysis Cure?* Chicago, IL: University of Chicago Press.

Kolb, D. A. (1984). *Experiential Learning: Experience as the Source of Learning and Development*. New Jersey: Prentice-Hall.

Kolb, D., & Frohman, A. (1970). An organization development approach to consulting. *Sloan Management Review*, 12, 1: 51–65.

Kolb, A. Y., & Kolb, D. A. (2010). Learning to play, playing to learn: A case study of a ludic learning space, *Journal of Organizational Change Management*, 23, 1: 26–50.

Krantz, J., & Maltz, M. (1997). A Framework for Consulting to Organizational Role, *Consulting Psychology: Practice and Research*, 49, 2: 137–151.

Lawrence, G. W. (1985). Management development ... some ideals, images and realities. In: A. D. Colman & M. H. Geller (Eds.), *Group Relations Reader 2* (pp. 231–241). Washington, DC: A. K. Rice Institute Series..

Levine, D. P. (2001). Know no limits: the destruction of self-knowledge in organizations, *Psychoanalytic Studies*, 3, 2: 237–245.

Levine, M. (1999). Rethinking bystander nonintervention: Social categorization and the evidence of witnesses at the James Bulger murder trial. *Human Relations*, 52, 9: 1133–1155.

Luft, J., & Ingham, H. (1955). The Johari window, a graphic model of interpersonal awareness. *Proceedings of the Western Training Laboratory in Group Development*. Los Angeles: UCLA.

Marris, P. (1982). Attachment and society. In: C. M. Parkes & J. Stevenson-Hinde (Eds.), *The Place of Attachment in Human Behaviour* (pp. 185–204). London: Tavistock Publications.

McCann, J. & Selsky, J. W. (1984). Hyperturbulence and the emergence of type V environments. *Academy of Managment Review*, 9: 460–470.

Mintzberg, H. (1991). The effective organization: Forces and forms, *MIT Sloan Management Review*.

Morgan, G. (1986). *Images of Organization*. London: Sage.

Ogden, T. H. (1992). *The Matrix of the Mind: Object Relations and the Psychoanalytic Dialogue*. London: Karnac.

Oliver, J. (1999). *The Naked Chef*. London: Penguin Books.

Owers, P. (2009). Consulting in hyperturbulent conditions to organisations in transition. In: S. Whittle & K. Izod (Eds.), *Mind-ful Consulting* (pp. 37–56). London: Karnac.

Parker, R. (2007). Killing the angel in the house; creativity, feminism and aggression. In: P. Williams & G. O. Gabbard (Eds.), *Key Papers in Literature and Psychoanalysis* (pp. 159–185). London: Karnac.

Polti, G. (1916). *The Thirty-Six Dramatic Situations*. Boston: The Writer Inc.

Power, M., Scheytt, T., Soin, K., & Sahlin, K. (2009). Reputational risk as a logic of organizing in late modernity, *Organization Studies, 30*: 301–324.

Reed, B. D., & Bazalgette, J. (2006). The organisational role analysis at the Grubb Institute of Behavioural Studies: origins and development. In: J. Newton, S. Long & B. Sievers (Eds.), *Coaching in Depth* (pp. 43–62). London: Karnac.

Rettie, R. (2005). Social presence as presentation of self. *Presence*, 357–358.

Riise, J. H. (2009). Organizational identity, identification and learning: how can organizations take advantage of the dynamic relationship between them. In: S. Whittle & K. Izod (Eds.), *Mind-ful Consulting* (pp. 19–36). London: Karnac.

Rustin, M. (1991). *The Good Society and the Inner World: Psychoanalysis, Politics and Culture*. London: Verso.

Sama, A. (2009). The use of history in organizational interventions. In: S. Whittle & K. Izod (Eds.), *Mind-ful Consulting* (pp. 181–198). London: Karnac.

Schein, E. (1990). *Organizational culture and leadership*. San Francisco, CA: Jossey-Bass.

Schein, E. (1999). *Process Consultation Revisited: Building the Helping Relationship*. Reading, MA: Addison-Wesley Publishing Company.

Schneider, K. (2008). *Existential-Integrative Psychotherapy: Guideposts to the Coreof Practice*. New York: Routledge.

Senge, P. (1994). *The 5th Discipline Fieldbook: Strategies for Building a Learning Organization*. New York: Nicholas Brealey Publishing.

Simpson, B., & Carroll, B. (2008). Re-viewing 'role' in processes of identity construction. *Organization, 15*, 1: 29–50.

Symington, N. (1993). *Narcissism: A New Theory*. London: Karnac.

Taleb, N. N. (2007). *The Black Swan: The Impact of the Highly Improbable*. London: Penguin.

Thorpe, R., & Moscorola, J. (1991). Detecting your research strategy. *Management Learning, 22*, 2: 127–133.

Tolbert, M., & Hannafin, J. (2006). Use of self in OD consulting: what matters is presence. In: B. B. Jones & M. Brazzel (Eds.), *The NTL handbook of organization development and change* (pp. 69–82). San Francisco: Pfeiffer.

Trist, E. L., Higgin, G., Mura, H. Pollock, G. (1990). The assumption of ordinariness as a denial mechanism. In: *The Tavistock Anthologies: The Social Engagement of Social Science, Volume 2* (pp. 476–493). University of Pennsylvania Press.

Voller, D. (2010). Negative capability. *Contemporary Psychotherapy, 2*, 2.

Walsh, M., & Whittle, S. (2009). When consultants collaborate and when they do not. In: S. Whittle & K. Izod (Eds.), *Mind-ful Consulting* (pp. 95–116). London: Karnac.

Webb, L. (2013). *Resilience: How to Cope When Everything Around You Keeps Changing*. Chichester: Capstone Publishing.

Weick, K. E., & Quinn, R. E. (1999). Organizational change and development. *Annual Review of Psychology, 50*: 361–388.

Whittle, S. R. (2013). Quick, quick, slow: time and timing in organizational change. In: S. R. Whittle & R. C. Stevens (Eds.), *Changing Organizations from Within: Roles, Risks, and Consultancy Relationships* (pp. 95–109). Farnham: Gower.

Whittle, S., & Izod, K. (Eds.) (2009). *Mind-ful Consulting*. London: Karnac.

Winnicott, D. W. (1951). Transitional objects and transitional phenomena. In: *Playing and Reality*. Harmondsworth: Penguin, 1971.
Winnicott, D. W. (1953). Transitional objects and transitional phenomena. *International Journal of Psychoanalysis, 34*: 89–97.
Winnicott, D. W. (1957). *The Child, the Family, and the Outside World*. London: Tavistock Publications.
Winnicott, D. W. (1986). *Home is Where We Start From*. New York: W. W. Norton.
Wizard of Oz (1939). Metro-Goldwyn-Mayer films.
Woolf, V. (1931). *Killing the Angel in the House: Seven Essays*. London: Penguin Books. [1995].
Zell, D. (2003). Organizational change as a process of death, dying, and rebirth. *The Journal of Applied Behavioral Science*, 39, 1: 73–96.

INDEX

acting out 6
advocacy 100–101
Alder, A. 90
Anderson, H. 3, 64
Angel in the House 116
anxious (ambivalent) attachment patterns 86
anxious (avoidant) attachment patterns 86
Argyris, C. xviii, 95, 100
attachment patterns 85–86
attachment theory 85

Bartholomew, K. xx, 86, 117
Bateson, G. 78
Bazalgette, J. 56
Beech, N. 7
Benjamin, J. 43
Benne, K. 74
Benne, K. D. 74
Berg, D. N. 28, 41
Bion, W. R. 91
Block, P. 69, 82, 99
Bowlby, J. xviii, xx, 6, 85
Bridger, H. 134
Bulger, James 91
Burns, H. 7
bystander, the 91–92

Carroll, B. 55–56, 58
carry on regardless 79–80
change 89–117
    bystander, the 91–92
    change with presence preoccupations 90–91
    confidence 90–91
    control 102–104
    data selection and interpretation 100
    gap between knowing and doing 89–90
    inference 93–97
    narrative structures 107–110
    recognition 105–106
    reputational risk 110, 113–114
    revelation 114–115
    trekker, the 92–93
    understanding of 90
Cheung-Judge, Mee-Yan. xx, xxii, 121
Chin, R. 74
Clarke, S. xx, 18, 73
Cohen, W. M. 78
competition 35–37, 40, 70, 74–75, 97–101, 117
compulsive organisation 71
confidence 33–35
consecutive modules 133
control 37–44, 69, 77, 79, 102–105, 117

Crombie, A. 34, 79
Cummings, T. G. 65, 69, 74

de Caestecker, L. 7
depressive organisation 71
Diamond, M. A. 4, 34
Dick, P. K. 102
Django Unchained and real life violence 27
dramatic organisation 71

Emery, F. E. xviii, 79
emotions 115

fallacy 94–95
Fonagy, P. xx, 20
French, R. 91

Gergely, G. xx, 20
Gergen, K. J. 7
Giddens, A. 8, 12
Gill, J. 120
Goffman, E. xviii, 105
Grueneisen, V. 21, 69, 70

Hahn, H. xx, 18
Hannafin, J. 50
Harris, A. 57
Hatch, M. J. 81
Heron, J. 74
Higgin, G. 80
Hirschhorn, L. 32, 79, 110
Hoggett, P. xix–xx, 18, 77
Horney, K. 97–98
Horowitz, L. xx, 86, 117
Hunt, J. 125

Ibarra, H. 12
identity 73
    approach to professional development 15–16
    containment 21
    description 12–13
    inhabiting identities 11–12
    list 14
    makes itself felt in practice 17
    mirroring 19
    noticing emotional tendencies 23

preoccupations 64
projection and transference 22
recognition 17–18
regulation 19
revelation 21–22
signifiers 12
inaccurate inference 94
Ingham, H. 3
inquiry 100–101
Izod, K. xviii, xx, 10, 21, 57, 69–70, 119

Jacobs, M. L. 33
Johari window 3, 47
    analysis 4–5
Jung, C. G. 4
Jurist, E. L. xx, 20

Kahn, R. L. 32
Kahn, W. 28, 41, 46
Katz, D. 32
Kaye, J. 7
Kets de Vries, M. F. R. 71
Kirkpatrick, D. 83
Knowing me, knowing you 3–6
Kohut, H. 6
Kolb, A. Y. 8
Kolb, D. A. xx, 8
Krantz, J. 32, 56

Lawrence, G. W. 110
Levine, D. P. 98
Levine, M. 91
Levinthal, D. A. 78
Luft, J. 3

MacIntosh, R. 7
MacLean, D. 7
maladaptive strategies 79
Maltz, M. 32, 56
Management Today 120
Marris, P. xix, 15, 90
McCann, J. 120
Miller, D. 71
Miller, E. J. 71
Mind-ful Consulting 10, 119–120
Mintzberg, H. 103

Morgan, G. 71
Moscorola, J. 104
Mura, H. 80

"Naked Chef, The" 11
narrative plots 126

Ogden, T. H. 90
Oliver, J. 11
organisational models 71
Owers, P. xviii, 120

P3C
    activities 133–134
    as directors of 23
    learning out loud groups 24
    module themes 67, 129
    participants 8–9, 132
    presence in 29
    programme design 8–10, 29, 67, 129–131
paranoid organisation 71
Parker, R. 116
Petriglieri, J. L. 12
play 6
Pollock, G. 80
Polti, G. 126
potential space 1–2, 7–10, 30, 45, 54, 63, 73, 77, 90–91, 98, 101, 117, 121, 127, 130
Power, M. 109
practice
    assessment levels of change 84–85
    consulting cycle and 64–65
    dynamics of credibility and competition 70–72
    evaluations, exits and endings 81–83
    interventions and the dynamics of risk and accountability 74–78
    mixed emotions 69–70
    preoccupations 63
    stages of 65–66
presence
    about 28–31
    analytic streams of 43
    as intervention 50
    authority dynamics 32–33
    competition 35–37
    confidence 33–35
    control dynamics 39
    dynamics 37–39
    encounters and entanglements 44
    intended and unintended 41–42
    preoccupations 64
    presence index 40
    shapes 32
    transference 44–47
    traps 31
projection and transference 22–23
    mechanism 22
    successful 23

Quinn, R. E. xviii, 75

Reed, B. D. 56
regulation 17, 19–21, 24, 74, 77, 85, 109–114, 117
Rettie, R. 29
Riise, J. H. 80
role space 53–61
    analytic expectations 57
    applying 60
    configuration 54
    now and then, here and there 58
    realities of 55
    thinking my way 54–55
Rustin, M. 12, 19

Sahlin, K. 109
Sama, A. 9
Schein, E. 68, 74
Scheytt, T. 109
Schneider, K. 28
Schon, D. xviii
Schultz, M. 81
secure attachment patterns 85
self-as-instrument 9, 50, 121–123, 130
Selsky, J. W. 120
Senge, P. 95
shoddy armour 6
Simpson, B. 55–56, 58
Socio Psychological Perspective, The, *Socio Technical Perspective, The*, and *Socio Ecological, The* 130
Soin, K. 109
Symington, N. 5

Taleb, N. N. 73
Target, M. xx, 20
Tavistock Institute Practitioner Certificate in
    Consulting and Change Programme, The
    see P3C
Thorpe, R. 104
Tolbert, M. 50
transference 22–24, 44–47, 50
trekker, the 92–93
Trist, E. L. xviii, 79–80

Voller, D. 91

Walsh, M. 30, 99
Webb, L. 120
Weick, K. E. xviii, 75
western societies 35
Whittle, S. xviii, xx, 10, 30, 99, 119–120
Whittle, S. R. xx, 65
Winnicott, D. W. xviii, 1, 2, 5, 7–8, 130
Woolf, V. 115
Worley, C. G. 65, 69, 74

Zell, D. 75
zone of transition 2